Opposing Viewpoints®

POLLUTION

Other Books of Related Interest

Opposing Viewpoints®

POLLUTION

Louise I. Gerdes, *Book Editor*

Bruce Glassman, *Vice President*

Bonnie Szumski, *Publisher*

Helen Cothran, *Managing Editor*

OPPOSING
VIEWPOINTS®
SERIES

GREENHAVEN PRESS

An imprint of Thomson Gale, a part of The Thomson Corporation

THOMSON
———✳———™
GALE

Detroit • New York • San Francisco • San Diego • New Haven, Conn.
Waterville, Maine • London • Munich

THOMSON
GALE

For more information, contact
Greenhaven Press
27500 Drake Rd.
Farmington Hills, MI 48331-3535
Or you can visit our Internet site at http://www.gale.com

Greenhaven Press anthologies primarily consist of previously published material taken from a variety of sources, including periodicals, books, scholarly journals, newspapers, government documents, and position papers from private and public organizations. These original sources are often edited for length and to ensure their accessibility for a young adult audience. The anthology editors also change the original titles of these works in order to clearly present the main thesis of each viewpoint and to explicitly indicate the opinion presented in the viewpoint. These alterations are made in consideration of both the reading and comprehension levels of a young adult audience. Every effort is made to ensure that Greenhaven Press accurately reflects the original intent of the authors included in this anthology.

LIBRARY OF CONGRESS CATALOGING-IN-PUBLICATION DATA

Pollution / Louise I. Gerdes, book editor.
    p. cm. — (Opposing viewpoints series)
    Includes bibliographical references and index.
    ISBN 0-7377-2949-X (lib. : alk. paper) — ISBN 0-7377-2950-3 (pbk. : alk. paper)
      1. Pollution. 2. Pollution—Health aspects. 3. Pollution prevention. I. Gerdes,
Louise I., 1953– . II. Opposing viewpoints series (Unnumbered)
    TD176.7.P636 2006
    363.73—dc22
                                   2005045983

Printed in the United States of America

Contents

Why Consider Opposing Viewpoints?

"The only way in which a human being can make some approach to knowing the whole of a subject is by hearing what can be said about it by persons of every variety of opinion and studying all modes in which it can be looked at by every character of mind. No wise man ever acquired his wisdom in any mode but this."

John Stuart Mill

In our media-intensive culture it is not difficult to find differing opinions. Thousands of newspapers and magazines and dozens of radio and television talk shows resound with differing points of view. The difficulty lies in deciding which opinion to agree with and which "experts" seem the most credible. The more inundated we become with differing opinions and claims, the more essential it is to hone critical reading and thinking skills to evaluate these ideas. Opposing Viewpoints books address this problem directly by presenting stimulating debates that can be used to enhance and teach these skills. The varied opinions contained in each book examine many different aspects of a single issue. While examining these conveniently edited opposing views, readers can develop critical thinking skills such as the ability to compare and contrast authors' credibility, facts, argumentation styles, use of persuasive techniques, and other stylistic tools. In short, the Opposing Viewpoints Series is an ideal way to attain the higher-level thinking and reading skills so essential in a culture of diverse and contradictory opinions.

In addition to providing a tool for critical thinking, Opposing Viewpoints books challenge readers to question their own strongly held opinions and assumptions. Most people form their opinions on the basis of upbringing, peer pressure, and personal, cultural, or professional bias. By reading carefully balanced opposing views, readers must directly confront new ideas as well as the opinions of those with whom they disagree. This is not to simplistically argue that everyone who reads opposing views will—or should—change his or her opinion. Instead, the series enhances readers' understanding of their own views by encouraging confrontation with opposing ideas. Careful examination of others' views can lead to the readers' understanding of the logical inconsistencies in their own opinions, perspective on why they hold an opinion, and the consideration of the possibility that their opinion requires further evaluation.

Evaluating Other Opinions

To ensure that this type of examination occurs, Opposing Viewpoints books present all types of opinions. Prominent spokespeople on different sides of each issue as well as well-known professionals from many disciplines challenge the reader. An additional goal of the series is to provide a forum for other, less known, or even unpopular viewpoints. The opinion of an ordinary person who has had to make the decision to cut off life support from a terminally ill relative, for example, may be just as valuable and provide just as much insight as a medical ethicist's professional opinion. The editors have two additional purposes in including these less known views. One, the editors encourage readers to respect others' opinions—even when not enhanced by professional credibility. It is only by reading or listening to and objectively evaluating others' ideas that one can determine whether they are worthy of consideration. Two, the inclusion of such viewpoints encourages the important critical thinking skill of objectively evaluating an author's credentials and bias. This evaluation will illuminate an author's reasons for taking a particular stance on an issue and will aid in readers' evaluation of the author's ideas.

It is our hope that these books will give readers a deeper understanding of the issues debated and an appreciation of the complexity of even seemingly simple issues when good and honest people disagree. This awareness is particularly important in a democratic society such as ours in which people enter into public debate to determine the common good. Those with whom one disagrees should not be regarded as enemies but rather as people whose views deserve careful examination and may shed light on one's own.

Thomas Jefferson once said that "difference of opinion leads to inquiry, and inquiry to truth." Jefferson, a broadly educated man, argued that "if a nation expects to be ignorant and free . . . it expects what never was and never will be." As individuals and as a nation, it is imperative that we consider the opinions of others and examine them with skill and discernment. The Opposing Viewpoints Series is intended to help readers achieve this goal.

David L. Bender and Bruno Leone,
Founders

Introduction

*"We are what we pee. The 281 million citizens of the
United States are going to be peeing (and then drinking)
each other's medicines and personal care products for the
foreseeable future."*

—Mark D. Uehling, science writer

In 2002 the United States Geological Survey (USGS) published the results of a study that documented the chemical
contents of 139 rivers and streams nationwide. Several science magazines cited the study as one of the top science stories of the year. What the study revealed that was so remarkable was that the rivers and streams that feed America's water
supply contain antibiotics, antidepressants, birth control
substances, seizure medication, cancer treatments, pain-
killers, tranquilizers, and cholesterol-lowering compounds.
David Deslak, an engineer at the University of California at
Berkeley, claims, "There are 129 widely used drugs in municipal wastewater nationwide, 49 at levels above a key cut-
off point for potential regulation." In addition to prescription drugs, the study found that U.S. rivers and streams
contain ibuprofen, bug spray, sunscreen, mouthwash, an-
tibacterial soap, and other personal care products. Analysts
have dubbed these new pollutants "pharmaceuticals and personal care products" (PPCPs).

Unlike well-known water pollutants such as mercury,
PPCPs do not enter America's waters from industrial sources.
"The contaminants come from our bladders and bowels, our
bathtub drains and kitchen sinks. As much as 90 percent of
anything the doctor orders you to swallow passes out of your
body and into your toilet," science writer Mark D. Uehling
maintains. While American sewage treatment removes many
contaminants, it does not remove or counteract the drugs
that people excrete. Following the release of the USGS report, many commentators expressed concern about the impact of water containing PPCPs. The subsequent controversy is illustrative of similar controversies in the pollution
debate. While environmental and health activists claim that

the potential long-term dangers of pollutants suggest the need for preventative action, some scientists and others contend that policies regarding pollutants should be based on sound science, not unknown dangers.

The concentrations of PPCPs in the water supply are in fact small. Journalist Lori Valigra claims, "These contaminants occur in such tiny amounts . . .—at most, a drop of ink in the largest tanker truck—that so far most do not seem to pose a danger." Many scientists agree. Chemical and environmental engineering professor Robert G. Arnold maintains, "At 2 [liters of water] per day, it would take more than 250 years to ingest the amount of ibuprofen in a single capsule of Motrin. . . . Exposure to PhACs [pharmaceutically active compounds] via ingestion of water is negligible in comparison to medically administrated doses."

Environmental and health activists acknowledge that the concentrations of PPCPs are small. They are nevertheless concerned about the cumulative and long-term risks. "Drugs are designed to have an effect in small quantities and small amounts of different chemicals can add up or interact," argues Women and Health Protection (WHP), a Canadian women's health organization. Theo Colborn, senior scientist at the World Wildlife Fund (WWF) and author of *Our Stolen Future*, an oft-cited book advocating caution concerning chemical contaminants, is concerned about synthetic hormones that may mix with other chemicals already present in streams. "You can liken it to side effects of a prescription drug—you don't know how it's going to interact with the over-the-counter drugs you're taking," Colborn argues. "It's the unexpected, interactive effects that are a real concern," she claims.

Researchers have in fact discovered a connection between PPCP-polluted waters and marine animal reproductive health. James Levitt of the University of Minnesota compared walleyed pike upstream with those found downstream. The male fish swimming in the polluted downstream water had no sperm and had malformed testes; the downstream female fish had degenerated ovaries. According to Uehling, "Researchers point to a large number of other water-dwelling creatures that are having similar problems. Alligators, carp, otters, and other aquatic creatures are increasingly prone to disturbing defects or illnesses in their reproductive tracts."

In light of this evidence, activists urge a policy approach known as the precautionary principle. According to this principle, when scientists suspect potential threats to human health or the environment, they recommend taking action to prevent possible harm although scientific evidence may not yet be conclusive. WHP argues, "Marine life deformities tell us PPCPs have already affected the ecosystem on which we depend. We need to act now, to reverse these problems and to prevent others."

Those who oppose precautionary, preventive measures contend that the uncertainty about the impact of PPCPs suggests the need for further research, not irrational spending to control unknown risks. Professor Arnold claims that current research is insufficient to warrant action. "The expense of widespread additional wastewater treatment to regulate levels of endocrine disrupting compounds in our surface water resources is not warranted based on what we know," he claims. Arnold argues that policy priorities based on speculation threaten programs that protect people from known harms. "Some environmental regulations have distorted spending on behalf of the public so that we seem unable to provide universal health care, adequate child-care services, and uniformly good public education," Arnold asserts. Objections to preventive action also come from doctors, farmers, and consumers who do not want to part with their medicines and personal care products, some commentators claim. Uehling asserts:

> Even imagining a cosmic political shift—a realignment after which environmentalists wrestled the drug and chemical companies into submission—the do-gooders would still have an insurmountable hurdle. They would have to contend with doctors and farmers and soccer moms who love their drugs, their hormones, their cleaning products. Would you want to give up your favorite deodorant? What if the best medicine for your toddler had to be withdrawn to protect the damned environment?

These opposing views—that pollution policies should emphasize caution and, alternatively, that pollution policies should be postponed until evidence of actual harm is found—

shape nearly every pollution debate. These views can be seen in the controversies presented in the following chapters of *Opposing Viewpoints: Pollution:* Is Pollution a Serious Problem? Does Pollution Threaten Public Health? How Can Society Reduce Pollution? What Government Policies Would Reduce Pollution? To be sure, the uncertainty over the impact of PPCPs in America's water supply remains. Professor Arnold, an analyst who opposes preventive action, contends that "human health effects from exposure to estrogenic compounds are entirely speculative at this point." Nevertheless, he concedes that "effects about which there has been speculation—rising rates of breast cancer and broadly declining sperm counts— are potentially calamitous."

CHAPTER 1

Is Pollution a Serious Problem?

Chapter Preface

When nations in the developing world enter the global economy, they not only gain its benefits, they also face its challenges, including the problem of air pollution. The editors of *Geographical* note, for example, that "as Asia, the world's most populated region, has undergone rapid economic development, there has been a concomitant growth in the problem of air pollution. The result is an extraordinary three-kilometre-deep brown cloud that regularly develops over much of the continent. This thick haze is caused by dramatic increases in emissions from vehicles, industries and power stations." While some observers see air pollution in the developing world as a serious problem, others are optimistic it will improve.

Regardless of whether critics see the problem in positive or negative terms, most agree that air pollution in the developing world has increased substantially. Author Daniel Litvin describes the problem:

> On Cold days in Delhi [India], the poor light bonfires of tyres, trees and rags whose fumes mix with the exhaust from the city's . . . vehicles to form a thick smog. On most days in Mexico City, a blanket of pollution cuts off views of the surrounding mountains. On one famous occasion it got so bad that birds fell dead out of the sky on to the Zocalo, the city's main square. . . . The air in Asia's cities, like the water in its rivers, is particularly unhealthy, containing levels of dust and smoke several times higher than in the rich countries' cities.

This air pollution poses a serious threat to the health of people in the developing world, many analysts claim. Of greatest concern is small particle pollution, caused by vehicle exhaust, coal burning, smoke from factories, and dust stirred up by vehicles, all of which end up in people's lungs, particularly those who live in urban areas. EnviroFit, an organization whose goal is to distribute pollution-reduction technologies in developing countries, maintains, "A study in India estimated that air pollution caused 37,000 premature deaths in the seven cities studied, increasing 50% in a 5 year period. In Manila, a recent World Bank study estimated that the annual health cost of human exposure to particulate matter (PM10) was US $430 million." For many, this toll on human health indicates that immediate action is necessary to reduce dangerous air pollution in developing nations.

Some commentators are also concerned about the air pollution produced in developing countries that is drifting toward the United States. "Environmentalists in the developed world also worry about air pollution in poorer countries, not just out of the goodness of their hearts but because they fear it may affect their own backyard," Litvin contends. Some argue that this transborder air pollution will make it difficult for U.S. states to meet air-pollution reduction goals. "Ozone from China readily crosses the Pacific during spring, raising the concentrations of this pollutant across the United States," *Science News* maintains. This pollution migration, the magazine contends, makes "it harder for states to meet federal air quality standards."

However, some observers are optimistic about air pollution in the developing world. For example, statistician Bjorn Lomborg, whose controversial book *The Skeptical Environmentalist* disputes claims that the environment is threatened, questions whether air pollution in the developing world is a serious problem. In his article "The Developed World Is Cleaner Than Ever," Lomborg argues, "The air of the Western world has not been as clean as it is now for a long time, and there is good reason to assume that air pollution in the developing world will also improve with time." Lomborg contends that the impressive improvements in air quality made by developed nations will also occur in the developing world. He asserts, "Not only have we seen that air pollution can—and historically has been—combated in the developed world. There is also good reason to believe that the developing world, following our pattern, in the long run likewise will bring down its air pollution."

Lomborg's optimism is obviously not shared by everyone. Those concerned about the health of the people in developing nations contest his positive view of pollution in developing nations. The authors in the following chapter explore other controversies in the pollution debate to determine whether pollution is a serious problem or whether more optimism concerning this issue is warranted.

"Our air is polluted. Our soil is contaminated. Our water is poisoned."

Pollution Is a Serious Problem

Ruth Gadebusch

Industries that provide food, energy, and other products for human consumption are polluting the air, soil, and water, argues Ruth Gadebusch in the following viewpoint. Most Americans know that coal burning factories, agricultural dust, nuclear power plants, and vehicle emissions all contribute to pollution, she contends, yet people continue to consume without taking responsibility for the results. Gadebusch is a syndicated columnist.

As you read, consider the following questions:
1. According to Gadebusch, why did America go to war against Iraq?
2. What kinds of dirty air can people do nothing about, in the author's opinion?
3. In the author's view, what is still dumped into our rivers and oceans?

Ruth Gadebusch, "Squandering Our Future," *Liberal Opinion Week*, September 6, 2003. Copyright © 2003 by Pythian Press. Reproduced by permission.

Our air is polluted. Our soil is contaminated. Our water is poisoned. And on, and on, and on. Just what kind of heritage are we leaving our descendants? It's pay now, or pay later.

For some years now we have known of the damage we are doing to our planet but we refuse to deal with the problems. We seem to have the philosophy of "eat, drink and be merry for tomorrow you may die." It is true that at some point we will all die but that doesn't relieve us of the responsibility for the time that we do spend here.

The Sources of Pollution

For many of us it is beyond suspicion that this nation went to war against a Middle Eastern country [Iraq] more for its black gold than to liberate a downtrodden people. It is this oil that fuels the vehicles that are major contributors to our bad air, not to forget the contamination dropped on-to and-in-to the ground around the refineries.

Not to put all the blame on oil, it is well known that particles generated from coal burning factories in the Northeastern United States travel many, many miles south. In my state, California, with the dubious distinction of having more than its fair share of polluted air, it is agriculture plowing stirring up dust and burning of waste pouring smoke into the air, along with the great number of miles traveled using the internal combustion engine.

We may not be able to do anything about the dirty air resulting from Mother Nature's flare-ups like tornados, volcanic eruptions and such but we surely could counteract the actions of humankind. When the pressure is on we have generally found alternatives. Some of our energy needs could surely be met through wind and solar use.

Both wind and sun are plentiful in many parts of our nation and around the world. We simply have to make the commitment. Of course we need to think it through rather thoroughly and avoid such boondoggles as putting windmills in a major bird flyaway as happened in Southern California.

We have contaminated our soil with all sorts of chemicals poured into the ground. For years we never stopped to think about where the stuff that we dumped was going and just how much the ground could absorb. We didn't worry about leaking containers of various poisons. Now we find that to clean up the soil is a monumental undertaking and a problem of just where to put the contaminated materials. None of us want it in our back yard.

Golliver. © 1997 by Gary Oliver. Reproduced by permission.

We still do not have a very satisfactory solution of just what to do with radioactive leftovers from our nuclear generating plants. In addition the neighbors of the plants that generated the radioactive waste live in fear of accidents filling the air with contamination.

Our daily garbage collection is another matter of concern. Sewage in various stages of cleanliness, and not so clean, still gets dumped into our rivers and oceans. Many places in the world have no sanitation whatsoever. Many of these same areas around the world as well as in our nation are having increasing difficulty supplying clean water to the people.

A Demand for Water
This latter is due to a number of different factors including an increasing population that chooses to live in water-short

areas. Our living standards demand great quantities of water. I remember in rural Georgia when electricity brought us pumped water we had to increase the size of our well because a lot more was used when one cut on a faucet rather than drawing it up by the bucket.

I still see many people leave faucets running because it is easier than to cut it off and on as needed, or just let gallons pour out waiting for the hot water. Then there are the dripping faucets. Much of our Southwestern US, naturally desert, has been made to bloom. Beautiful, but is it the best use of this limited resource?

We are desecrating our environment in so many ways with so little thought given to the future. We just want to enjoy ourselves and leave the bill for someone else. Our current administration instead of leading the way with conservation has gone in the opposite direction. Have we no conscience?

To make matters worse we are short-changing the education our children need in order to find solutions to the messes we have made and continue to make. While an individual undoubtedly benefits from education the true benefit accrues to the society.

In our present economic crisis we are saying we cannot afford to do some of the more expensive alternatives to our wasteful life-styles. The truth is we can ill afford not to. Most assuredly the answer is not in making it more difficult for our children to get an education. New York has just increased fees for its public institutions of higher education by 28%. In California it is 30%. In Arizona it is a whopping 39% increase. All these increases were done with little or no time for students to prepare for additional fees.

There will be a day of reckoning for our shortsightedness. We can make some sacrifices ourselves or we can continue to postpone the inevitable. It just depends on what kind of heritage we want to pass on.

> *"We have made huge progress in purifying industrial and municipal waste before it is emitted."*

Pollution Is Not a Serious Problem

Stephen Moore

Contrary to the claims of environmental doomsayers, American industrialization and consumption have not led to deteriorating air and water quality, claims Stephen Moore in the following viewpoint. In fact, argues Moore, economic growth leads to affluence, and wealthy societies have more resources to combat pollution. U.S. economic development and advanced technology have led to cleaner air and water, and contributed to more efficient waste disposal and energy consumption, he maintains. Moore, former president of the Club for Growth, a free-market public policy organization, is a contributing editor of *National Review*.

As you read, consider the following questions:
1. In Moore's opinion, what is the most environmentally friendly invention in world history?
2. According to the author, what is one of the most gratifying environmental success stories in recent years?
3. What is the most precious resource of all, in the author's view?

There is almost certainly no issue of modern times in which Americans' general beliefs about the state of affairs is so contrary to objective reality than in the area of the environment. Most Americans believe that because of industrialization, population growth and mass consumption, our air and our water are deteriorating and that our access to natural resources will soon run dry. We read stories about global warming, ozone depletion and the paving over of the planet and think that the environment must have been cleaner and more pristine 50 and 100 years ago.

The Real State of the Environment

In a recent poll, when Americans were asked what would be some of the greatest problems that mankind will confront over the next 50 years, the top two responses dealt with the environment. More than four of five said they feared "severe water pollution" and "severe air pollution" with three areas of environmental conditions: 1) air quality, 2) water quality and 3) availability of natural resources.

But here is the real state of the environment. Contrary to infamous doom and gloom reports of the 1960s and 1970s, we are not running out of energy, food, forests or minerals. The data clearly show that natural resource scarcity—as measured by cost or price—has been decreasing rather than increasing in the long run for all raw materials, energy and food, with only temporary exceptions. That is, resources have become more abundant, not less so. Even the U.S. government now apparently recognizes the errors of its judgments in the past. Reversing the forecasts of studies such as Global 2000, the Office of Technology Assessment in Technology and the American Transition has concluded: "The nation's future has probably never been less constrained by the cost of natural resources."

The major driving forces behind our improved environment are our greater access to natural resources, our affluence and our technology. Technological improvements and inventions have helped combat the worst kinds of pollution. The computer, for example, is arguably the most environmentally friendly invention in world history, by producing massive amounts of output with virtually no environmental costs. It is also true that a wealthier society is a healthier one. Wealthier societies can afford to devote more resources to combating pollution. We now know that the greatest environmental catastrophes of this century were caused by socialist nations. The communists in the Soviet Union were perhaps the greatest environmental villains in history. Prudent government regulation is necessary to protect the environment. But more important is a free market economy: one that protects property rights, produces wealth and encourages innovation. . . .

One of the major reasons we place a high premium on a clean and safe environment is for protection of our health. But every health trend has shown vast and uninterrupted improvement over the past century. The child death rate has fallen 20-fold. Life expectancy has leaped forward by 30 years in the U.S. and has nearly doubled in many developing nations such as India, China and Mexico. These statistics certainly call into question the premise that pollution is worse now than 50 or 100 years ago, given that the health of the world's population has so dramatically improved over this time period.

Measuring Air Quality

But let us look at more direct evidence on the amount of air pollution in the U.S. The prevailing attitude of Americans, amplified by the media and academia, is that the giant leaps forward in industrial production have come at the expense of degrading our air and water quality. In the 1960s Harvard economist John Kenneth Galbraith wrote in his bestseller, *The Affluent Society*, that a fundamental tension exists between environmental and economic progress. Former Vice President Al Gore wrote more contemporaneously in his book, *Earth in the Balance*, that we have been mortgaging our environmental future through our mindless pursuit of economic growth. The surprising good news is that the economic progress of the last century has not come at the expense of clean air. Rather, economic growth has generally corresponded with improvements in the natural environment.

The national picture on air quality shows improvement for almost every type of pollution. Lead concentrations have amazingly fallen by more than 90 percent since 1976. In fact, the total volume of lead emissions was lower in 1990 than in 1940 (the furthest back we have reliable data) and was lower than in every intervening year. According to a 1999 report by the Pacific Research Institute, based on EPA air quality data, between 1976 and 1998 sulfur dioxide levels decreased 66 percent, nitrogen oxides decreased 38 percent, ozone decreased 31 percent, carbon monoxide decreased 66 percent, and particulates decreased 25 percent (between 1988 and 1997).

Prosperity Is Compatible with a Cleaner Environment

Many environmentalists believe an industrial civilization is incompatible with a clean and safe environment. Yet the historical record on this point reveals just the opposite: Prosperity is a necessary precondition for environmental protection.
- Prosperous societies can afford to invest in environmental protection, and they do: The U.S. has spent over $1 trillion since 1970 on pollution abatement alone. Countries that are poor or have stagnant economies tend to be the worse polluters.
- Increasing economic efficiency—a key component of economic growth—is also the key to reducing pollution, since pollution is usually the result of the inefficient use of natural resources.

Joseph L. Bast, Peter J. Hill, and Richard O. Rue, *Eco-Sanity: A Common-Sense Guide to Environmentalism*, 1996.

What about the smog levels in particular high-pollution cities? It was just a bit over 30 years ago that doomsayer Paul Ehrlich wrote in *The Population Bomb*, that "smog disasters" might kill 200,000 people in New York or Los Angeles by 1973. The reality is that air pollution in American cities has been falling for at least the past three decades. For example, air pollution, or soot, over Manhattan has fallen by two-thirds since the end of World War II. Air pollution over Chicago, Denver, Philadelphia and Washington, D.C., declined by more than 50 percent between 1972 and 1996. Perhaps the most gratifying environmental success story in recent years has been the rapid reduction in smog levels over Los Angeles in just the past decade. From 1985 to 1995, the number of days in the year of unhealthy air quality has fallen from about 160 to about 80. Pittsburgh's air quality improvements over the past 40 years have been even more spectacular. In the 1920s, 30s, 40s and 50s, as the steel mills' smokestacks belched out black soot, there were typically more than 300 "smoky" days a year. Since the late 1960s, that number has fallen to about 60 smoky days a year.

Water Quality Trends

One measure of the improvement in water quality over this century has been the dramatic reduction in outbreaks of disease from drinking water. At the start of the century, many life-threatening illnesses, such as diarrhea, were a result of Americans drinking and using impure water. In fact, waterborne diseases were a leading cause of death in the 19th century. In the 1930s and 1940s there were about 25 waterborne disease outbreaks a year. Nowadays there are almost none.

Unfortunately, there is not much reliable long-term data on the pollution levels of American lakes and rivers. Official measurements come from the Environmental Protection Agency and start around 1960—a decade or so before the Clean Water Act was signed into law. Over the past quarter century our lakes, streams and rivers have become much less polluted, and the trend is toward continued improvement. Since 1970 an estimated $500 billion has been spent on water cleanup. That spending has apparently paid off. The percentage of water sources that were judged by the Council on Environmental Quality to be poor or severe fell from 30 percent in 1961 to 17 percent in 1974 to less than 5 percent today.

We have made huge progress in purifying industrial and municipal waste before it is emitted into streams, rivers, and lakes. In 1960 only 40 million Americans—22 percent of the population—were served by wastewater treatment plants. By 1996 that had risen to 190 million Americans, or 72 percent of the population. One consequence of these gains is that many streams, rivers and lakes which were at one time severely polluted are now much more pristine. . . .

Price hikes in oil and electricity have also renewed calls in Washington, D.C., for a greater emphasis on energy efficiency in the workplace and at home. Environmentalists portray Americans as irresponsible over-consumers of energy. Wrong. The United States today may well be the most energy-efficient society in the history of man. Energy efficiency continued to surge so much in the 1990s that today we produce almost twice as much output per unit of energy as in the first half of this century. One often overlooked benefit of the digital and the information age is the huge gain registered in energy efficiency in the world economy.

Economic development and free markets are the keys to increasing energy efficiency. In 1986, a few years before the collapse of the Berlin Wall, the U.S. and other developed countries used less than half the amount of energy per dollar of GDP (Gross Domestic Product) than did the socialist economies. Communist North Korea still uses roughly three times as much energy to produce a dollar output than does South Korea.

Our modern society has also become much more efficient in waste disposal. Solid waste in the U.S. slightly more than doubled from 1960 to 1990. Yet over this same time period the amount of recycling rose by 96 percent. About 70 percent, a record high, of physical waste now generated in America is biodegradable. . . .

All of this is to say that the gains in environmental progress and resource abundance are a result of the most precious resource of all: the human intellect. This is the primary reason that we should be optimistic that the gains that have been made in the past 100 years will continue in the 21st century rather than reverse themselves. This is because almost all of the progress noted in the previous sections is primarily the result of the wondrous advances in the storehouse of human knowledge that has accumulated in this century.

We now stand on the shoulders of our ancestors, able to draw upon the accumulated knowledge and know-how of the past two centuries. This knowledge is our communal wealth. Much more than the power to enjoy gadgets, our wealth represents the power to mobilize nature to our advantage, rather than to just accept the random fates of nature. We now have all the evidence at hand to say definitively that Malthus[1] was *wrong*, and so were his legions of modern-day doomsday followers.

---

1. Thomas Malthus is famous for his hypothesis that unchecked population growth would exceed the food supply. Malthus concluded that unless family size was regulated, famine would become globally epidemic and eventually consume humankind.

"More people may die prematurely as a result of exposure to minute particles in the air than die in accidents on the highway."

Air Pollution Remains a Threat

Peter Jaret

Airborne particulate pollution remains a serious problem, asserts Peter Jaret in the following viewpoint. Although the larger, more obvious particulate pollution has been addressed, tiny airborne dust particles that come from industrial and vehicle emissions, construction sites, and farms continue to threaten human health, he claims. According to Jaret, this form of particulate pollution is not an urban problem alone; in fact, diesel-powered vehicles on dirty rural roads produce more particulate pollution than vehicles on city roads. Experts must seek new strategies to deal with this kind of pollution, he contends. Jaret is a frequent contributor to *National Wildlife* and *Health* magazines.

As you read, consider the following questions:

1. According to the Natural Resources Defense Council, how many Americans will die from health problems brought on by breathing concentrations of airborne dust?
2. What did Ann Miguel's team find in the dust vacuumed off Southern California byways?
3. In Jaret's opinion, what are the dangers of the "fugitive dust" whipped into Phoenix, Arizona, air?

Peter Jaret, "Why Tiny Particles Pose Big Problems," *National Wildlife*, vol. 39, February/March 2001. Copyright © 2001 by the National Wildlife Federation. Reproduced by permission.

[In 1999] if you had driven along certain residential streets in Long Beach or Los Angeles, you might have seen Ann Miguel pushing a vacuum cleaner down the center of the road. No, she's not an obsessive neatnik. A scientist at California Institute of Technology, Miguel is one of a growing number of researchers studying an environmental threat all around us: dust.

The Dangers of Dust

Dust is not just the collection of lint that drifts into the corners of your rooms. Tiny particles, often called particulate matter, are swept up by passing car tires, blown into the wind from construction sites and farms and spewed into the air by tail pipes and power plants. And experts say there is growing evidence that all this dust and soot may cause serious health problems—not only for humans but for other species as well.

One alarm sounded [in the summer of 2000] when a comparison of levels of particulate matter and death rates in the nation's 90 largest metropolitan areas was released. The study, conducted by scientists at the Johns Hopkins University School of Public Health, found that for every cubic meter of air, an increase of 20 micrograms of airborne particulate matter (that's a scant 70 millionths of an ounce) brought a 1 percent rise in the death rate. Hospital admissions for elderly people exposed to the increased pollution rose between 2 and 4 percent.

These troubling findings are just the latest danger sign. "Once we got rid of most of the big, obvious nasty stuff in the air during the 1970s and 1980s, we thought we had addressed the particulate-matter problem," says John Vandenberg, director of the National Particulate Matter Research Program at the U.S. Environmental Protection Agency (EPA). "Then in the early 1990s studies came along that knocked us back on our heels." In one, the nonprofit Natural Resources Defense Council calculated that as many as 60,000 Americans die each year from lung diseases, heart conditions and other health problems brought on by breathing concentrations of airborne dust. More people may die prematurely as a result of exposure to minute particles in the air than die in accidents on the highway, experts now think.

Where Do the Particles Come From?

The particles of greatest concern are 10 microns or less in diameter. (A human hair, by comparison, is about 70 microns thick.) Dust motes that spin in the air when the sun pours in the window measure roughly 10 microns. The much smaller airborne bits that make up cigarette smoke are only about half a micron or less in diameter—so small that instead of seeing individual particles you perceive a cloud of them concentrated together. About 60 percent of particulate matter 10 microns or less in size comes from combustion sources, such as cars and power plants. The rest come from construction, agriculture and particles stirred into the air by passing cars on the nation's roads and highways.

When Miguel and her team analyzed road dust vacuumed off byways of Southern California using a standard Shop-Vac, they found soil, deposited motor vehicle exhaust, pollens, animal dander, even minute particles from brake linings and tires. Scientists have also identified heavy metals, cancer-causing toxic substances, bacteria and viruses in airborne dust.

The problem of particulate pollution isn't limited to cities and suburbs. Jay Turner, an engineer at Washington University in St. Louis, set up monitors on both an urban interstate and a rural Illinois road. The average urban vehicle generates between 30 and 40 milligrams of particulate matter per mile traveled, he found. The average rural vehicle sends between 200 to 300 milligrams into the air. The reason: There is more soil dust on rural roads and more diesel-powered vehicles.

The Impact on the Lungs

Those particles can cause breathing problems. In 1999, British researchers exposed 15 volunteers to air mixed with diesel exhaust particles for the period of one hour—about the level you would inhale on a smoggy day in Los Angeles. Six hours later, the scientists found signs of inflammation in the lungs. In another experiment, researchers from the University of Texas-Houston Health Science Center exposed immune cells called macrophages to ash collected from the Mount St. Helen's eruption and to airborne dust from St. Louis and Washington, D.C. Volcanic dust had no effect on the cells.

The urban dust, on the other hand, caused macrophages that normally keep immune reactions under control to die. The result: overly aggressive immune responses that cause inflammatory damage to the lungs.

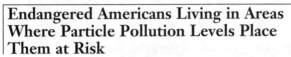

Endangered Americans Living in Areas Where Particle Pollution Levels Place Them at Risk

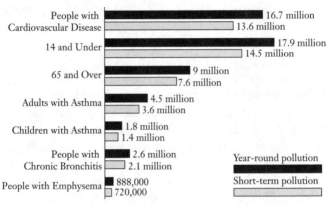

	Year-round pollution	Short-term pollution
People with Cardiovascular Disease	16.7 million	13.6 million
14 and Under	17.9 million	14.5 million
65 and Over	9 million	7.6 million
Adults with Asthma	4.5 million	3.6 million
Children with Asthma	1.8 million	1.4 million
People with Chronic Bronchitis	2.6 million	2.1 million
People with Emphysema	888,000	720,000

American Lung Association, "State of the Air: 2004," 2004.

Researchers think that inhaled particles can cause asthmatic attacks and may pose a serious threat to elderly patients whose lungs are already weakened by age and illness. Babies and young children are also at increased risk; per pound of body weight, they inhale more particulates than adults.

Putting Demands on the Heart

Lung problems are not the only worry. There is new evidence that tiny particles—from diesel trucks, cars, industrial plants and even windblown dust—also alter normal heart rate and rhythm. A healthy heart is able to vary its beats per minute widely, depending on the demands being placed on the body. But when researchers at Harvard Medical School took electrocardiogram and blood-pressure readings from 21 Boston residents over age 50, heart rate variability decreased dramatically when levels of very fine particulate matter in the air were high. "That's worrisome, because decreased heart rate variability is known to be a risk factor for sudden heart failure," says the EPA's Vandenberg.

Why tiny inhaled particles impact heartbeat is anyone's guess. "One possibility is that when you inhale these very small particles deep into your lungs, some of them make their way into the bloodstream, where they would tend to reach organs that process a lot of blood, such as the heart," says University of Delaware environmental scientist Anthony Wexler, who has studied how very small particulates make their way into the lungs. "The particles could then become lodged in cardiac muscle, reducing blood flow and affecting heart rhythm." According to one estimate, particulates are responsible for 1 percent of all heart disease fatalities in the United States, or about 10,000 deaths a year.

Virtually no one has looked at the effects of airborne particles on wildlife, although many laboratory studies show that inhaled dust can damage both the hearts and lungs of dogs, mice and other animals. In one investigation, dogs exposed to levels of particulates no higher than those found in many U.S. cities experienced significant changes in their heart rhythms. And [in 2000], scientists at Duke University warned that increasing amounts of atmospheric dust from the prolonged drought in the Sahel region of Africa have begun to threaten coral reefs in different parts of the planet. The dust, which is five times as thick as normal due to the dry spell, contains bacteria, viruses and fungi. Included is a soil fungus called Aspergillus that has killed more than 90 percent of the Caribbean's sea fans, a form of soft coral.

Reducing Exposure to Dust

There is little scientists can do to block dust storms whipped up by drought conditions, of course. But as worry over the health effects of airborne particles increases, experts are looking for ways to reduce exposure levels. The EPA is making a major effort to clean up diesel exhaust, which is a large contributor to particulate levels. In California, researchers at the University of California-Davis have developed a novel way to "fingerprint" dust in order to trace its source. The technique, which identifies unique mixtures of soil bacteria and fungi, may be used eventually to enforce regulations that limit the amount of dust kicked up by agricultural operations.

Indeed, airborne dust may become a rallying cry for those opposed to development. In Phoenix [Arizona], one of the biggest sources of air pollution is "fugitive dust," whipped into the air by the area's booming new housing tracts. The dust poses a special danger because it has been shown to contain a fungus called Coccidioides immitis, which normally resides in the soil. Once inhaled, the fungus causes valley fever. Symptoms resemble a bad case of the flu, but if the fungus spreads from the lungs into other parts of the body, the disease can be fatal.

Luckily there are a few simple ways to reduce your exposure to particulates. First, heed warnings to stay indoors during days when air pollution levels are high—especially if you suffer from asthma, respiratory allergies or heart disease. If you exercise outdoors, schedule your workouts for early morning or in the evening, when particulate levels are generally lowest. Avoid jogging on streets with heavy traffic. If you find yourself driving behind a diesel-powered vehicle, leave extra open space between your car and the exhaust belching into the air ahead. At home, filters on heating and air-conditioning systems help remove dust from indoor air, as long as they are cleaned and maintained regularly.

"Public fears over air pollution are out of all proportion to the actual risks posed by current air pollution levels."

The Problem of Air Pollution Is Exaggerated

Joel Schwartz

Emission levels are dropping and U.S. air quality is improving, argues Joel Schwartz in the following viewpoint. Nevertheless, he contends, Americans believe that air pollution is a serious problem because environmental and health activists exaggerate air pollution levels. For example, the American Lung Association inflates regional pollution levels by combining pollution levels from cities that are actually miles apart, Schwartz claims. This leads Americans to conclude erroneously that people across the region are at risk when in fact air pollution may be high in only one city in the area, he maintains. Schwartz is a senior fellow at the Reason Public Policy Institute.

As you read, consider the following questions:

1. According to Schwartz, what will happen if people overestimate their exposure to and risk from air pollution?
2. Whom do Americans consider the most credible sources of information on the environment, in the author's opinion?
3. In the author's view, what will happen to per-mile emissions during the next twenty years?

Joel Schwartz, "Clearing of the Air," *Regulation*, Summer 2003. Copyright © 2003 by the Cato Institute. All rights reserved. Reproduced by permission.

The United States has made dramatic progress in reducing air pollution over the last few decades, and most American cities now enjoy relatively good air quality. But polls show that most Americans believe air pollution has grown worse or will become worse in the future, and that most people face serious risks from air pollution.

This disconnect between perception and reality is, in part, the result of environmental activists' exaggerations of air pollution levels and risks, which make air pollution appear to be increasing when in fact it has been declining. State and federal regulatory agencies sometimes also resort to such tasks, and the media generally report those claims uncritically. As a result, public fears over air pollution are out of all proportion to the actual risks posed by current air pollution levels, and there is widespread but unwarranted pessimism about the nation's prospects for further air pollution improvements.

If people overestimate their exposure to and risk from air pollution, they will demand stricter, more costly air pollution regulation. We face many threats to our health and safety, but have limited resources with which to address them; by devoting excessive resources to one exaggerated risk, we are less able to counter other genuinely more serious risks. People can make informed decisions about air pollution control only if they have accurate information on the risks they face.

Perception and Reality

The Environmental Protection Agency monitors ozone and other air pollutants at hundreds of locations around the United States. EPA has two ozone standards: The first, known as the "one-hour standard," requires that daily ozone levels exceed 125 parts per billion (ppb) on no more than three days in any consecutive three-year period. Ozone levels are determined based on hourly averages (hence the name of the standard). EPA's "eight-hour standard," promulgated in 1997, is more stringent. It requires that the average of the fourth-highest daily, eight-hour average ozone level from each of the most recent three years not exceed 85 ppb. The standards are difficult to compare because of their different forms, but the one-hour standard is roughly equivalent to an eight-hour standard set at about 95 ppb.

In the early 1980s, half of the nation's monitoring stations registered ozone in excess of the federal one-hour health standard, and they averaged more than 12 such exceedances per year. But as of the end of 2002, only 13 percent of the stations failed the one-hour standard and they averaged just four exceedances per year. . . . Even the most polluted areas of the country achieved impressive ozone reductions during the last 20 years. About 40 percent of monitoring locations currently exceed the more stringent eight-hour standard, but peak eight-hour ozone levels are also declining in most areas.

The nation's success with air quality extends beyond ozone to other pollutants. For example, between 1981 and 2000, carbon monoxide (CO) declined 61 percent, sulfur dioxide (SO_2) 50 percent, and nitrogen oxides (NO_x) 14 percent. Only two among hundreds of the nation's monitoring locations still exceed the CO and SO_2 standards. All areas of the country meet the NO_x standard. For all three pollutants, pollution levels are well below the EPA standards in almost all cases.

Emissions Are Dropping

Likewise, airborne particulate matter (PM) has also registered large declines. $PM_{2.5}$ (PM up to 2.5 microns in diameter) dropped 33 percent from 1980 to 2000, while the soot emissions rate from diesel trucks is down almost 85 percent since 1975.

This downward trend in pollution levels will continue. On-road pollution measurements show per-mile emissions from gasoline vehicles are dropping by about 10 percent per year as the fleet turns over to more recent models that start out and stay much cleaner than vehicles built years ago. Diesel truck emissions are also declining, albeit about half as fast. Although motorists are driving more miles each year and pollution growth means more motorists on the roads, the increases in driving are tiny compared to the large declines in vehicles emission rates and will do little to slow progress on auto pollution.

Emissions from industrial sources will also continue to drop. Starting in 2004, EPA regulations require a 60 percent reduction in warm-season NO_x emissions from coal-fired power plants and industrial boilers—the major industrial sources of ozone-forming pollution. The federal Clean Air Act requires a 20 percent reduction in PM-forming SO_2 from power plants between 2000 and 2010. Those reductions are in addition to substantial declines in industrial NO_x and SO_2 emissions over the last 30 years.

Examining the Misperceptions

Despite past success in reducing air pollution and the positive outlook for the future, polls show most Americans think air pollution is getting worse. For example:

- A January 2002 Wirthlin Poll found that 66 percent of Americans believe air pollution has gotten worse during the past 10 years, up from 61 percent two years before, while a poll commissioned by Environmental Defense in 2000 found that 57 percent of Americans believe environmental conditions have gotten worse during the last 30 years.
- Americans also believe that environmental quality will decline in the future. The 2000 Environmental Defense poll found that 67 percent of Americans believe air pollution will continue to get worse. Likewise, a March 2001 Gallup Poll found that 57 percent of Americans believe environmental quality is deteriorating. A 1999 *Washington Post* poll found that 51 percent of Americans believe pollution will greatly increase in the future, up from 44 percent in 1996. State-based surveys have found similar results. The Public Policy Institute of California recently reported that 78 percent of Californians believe the state has made only "some" or "hardly any" progress in solving environmental problems.
- Most Americans also believe air pollution is still a serious threat to their health. Some 80 percent of New Yorkers rate air pollution as a "very serious" or "somewhat serious" problem, as do 77 percent of Texans. When asked about the most serious environmental issue facing California, a 34 percent plurality chose air pollution, with "growth" coming in a distant second at 13 percent.

According to the old saying, "It's not the things we didn't know that hurt us; it's the things we knew for sure that turned out to be wrong." When it comes to air pollution, why do most Americans "know" so much that is not so? Americans consider environmental groups the most credible sources of information on the environment, yet those activist groups consistently provide misleading information on air pollution levels, trends, risks, and prospects. Americans also trust information from regulatory agencies, yet the agencies often paint a misleadingly pessimistic picture. At the same time, the media often provide extensive coverage of air pollution reports and press releases from environmentalists and government regulators, yet the press reports rarely include critical examination or context on the claims those organizations make.

Inflating Air Pollution Exposure

In its report "State of the Air 2003," the American Lung Association claimed that between 1999 and 2001, Los Angeles County averaged 35 days per year with ozone in excess of EPA's eight-hour ozone benchmark of 85 ppb. Yet, as shown in Figure 1, none of L.A. County's 14 ozone monitors regis-

Figure 1. L.A. Air

The American Lung Association's claim as to the air quality in Los Angeles County compared to the results from monitoring stations in various parts of the county.

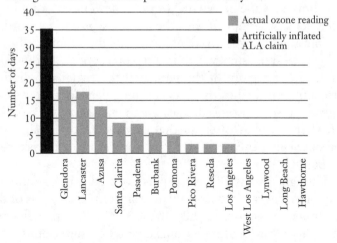

American Lung Association, "State of the Air: 2003," 2003.

tered anywhere near that many ozone exceedances. Indeed, the average L.A. County location averaged six exceedances per year—83 percent less than the report claims—while the most densely populated areas of the county never exceeded the EPA benchmark at all.

The American Lung Association derived its inflated value by assigning an ozone violation to the entire county on any day in which at least one location in the county exceeded 85 ppb. For example, if ozone was high one day in Glendora and the next day in Santa Clarita, 50 miles away, the reports counted two high-ozone days for all 9.5 million people in L.A. County. The logical fallacy here is obvious—it is like failing an entire class when one student does poorly. . . .

Regulatory agencies often take a similar tack in reporting ozone levels. For example, EPA recently downgraded California's San Joaquin Valley air district—a multi-county region—from "serious" to "severe" for the one-hour ozone standard. The change gave the region more time to attain the standard, but also required more stringent air pollution controls. In its press release on the action, EPA stated, "Air quality data from 1997 through 1999 indicated that San Joaquin Valley experienced 80 days of unhealthy levels of ozone air pollution." Yet Clovis, a suburb of Fresno and the most polluted location in the valley, had 40 days above the one-hour benchmark, while nearly half of the valley's monitoring locations actually complied with the one-hour ozone standard.

One might argue that talking about the number of days smog is elevated somewhere in a region is not misleading and paints a fair picture of the nature of the regional pollution problem. But the health effects of smog depend in how often a given person is exposed. Because no one is exposed to smog anywhere near as often as the activists' reports claim, the public is being encouraged to vastly overestimate its risk from air pollution.

Though dozens of newspapers covered one or more of those reports, most did not include any critical analysis of the proponents' assertions. Only about one in 10 papers flagged concerns regarding the fictional ozone exposure claims.

In the latest installment of its annual air pollution trends report, EPA claimed that 133 million Americans breathe air that exceeds one or more federal air pollution health standards—mainly the tough new annual $PM_{2.5}$ and eight-hour ozone standards. Yet EPA's claim is a substantial exaggeration.

The agency classifies Clean Air Act compliance status at the county level. For example, if any air pollution monitor in a county registers ozone in excess of federal requirements, that county is classified as "non-attainment." Regional classification often makes sense because pollution can be transported many miles from its source. The problem arises because EPA also uses county non-attainment status when counting the number of people who breathe polluted air. Because only one location in a county need exceed an air standard for the entire county to be classified as non-attainment, many people in a non-attainment county might still breathe clean air. Indeed, this situation is the norm, rather than the exception. . . .

The American Lung Association and PIRG [Public Interest Research Group] also exaggerate the geographic extent of high air pollution levels through misleading countywide, or even statewide, summaries of air pollution data. Indeed, most areas given an "F" grade for air quality by the American Lung Association actually comply with EPA's one-hour ozone standard, and many comply with the more stringent eight-hour standard. . . .

The Future Is Clear

Although often unacknowledged by environmentalists, America's past success in combating air pollution actually occurred in spite of rapid growth in vehicle travel. For example, the substantial pollution reduction achieved since 1980 occurred at the same time that total vehicle-miles increased 75 percent. But can improvements in vehicle pollution control keep pace with increased vehicle use?

Environmentalists seem to think that pollution from vehicles will inevitably increase. They cite rising population, increased vehicle travel, and the popularity of sport-utility vehicles (SUVs), and conclude that air pollution will therefore increase in the future. For example, in "Clearing the Air with Transit Spending," the Sierra Club asserts that past pollution improvements are now being "canceled out" by SUVs and suburban development. Environmentalists appear to be unaware that technological progress is reducing automobile emissions far more rapidly than driving is increasing. . . .

Based on observed emission trends and the requirements of new regulations, per-mile emissions will decline about 90 percent during the next 20 years, as twenty-first century vehicles make up an ever-larger portion of the fleet. Thus, even if Americans drive, say, 50 percent more miles 20 years from now (a greater increase than most metro areas project), total emissions would still decline by 85 percent from current levels.

Despite the evidence of substantial ongoing emission reductions from all major pollution sources, the American Lung Association asserts in its "State of the Air: 2003" report that "much air pollution cleanup has been stalled during the past five years" because of a lack of effort by EPA.

The Dose Makes the Poison

Both the number of people affected by air pollution and the severity of the effects decline with decreasing exposure. Exposure depends not only on ambient pollution levels, but also on time spent outdoors and level of physical activity. . . .

Environmental activists exaggerate the frequency and geographic extent of harmful pollution levels and also blur the distinction in health risk between modest and severe pollution problems. That misleads Americans to expect serious and permanent harm from current, relatively low levels of air pollution. For example, in "State of the Air," the American Lung Association asserts that 40 percent of Americans are "at risk" from ozone and suffer serious health damage even when ozone barely exceeds the eight-hour, 85 ppb benchmark just a few times per year, in spite of health research suggesting that this is a vast exaggeration.

PIRG's "Danger in the Air" declares without qualification that "our cities, suburbs and even our national parks are shrouded in smog for much of the summer," while the American Lung Association decries "the smog that regularly blankets many urban areas during the summer months," implying that most people are frequently exposed to air pollution at levels that could cause permanent harm. In reality, among areas exceeding federal ozone standards, the average location exceeds the one-hour benchmark about four times a year and the eight-hour benchmark about 11 times a year. Most areas of the United States now meet federal ozone standards, and high ozone levels have become infrequent in most areas that do exceed the standards.

"*Of all the pollutants released into the environment every year by human activity [persistent organic pollutants] are among the most dangerous.*"

Persistent Organic Pollutants Are a Serious Problem

Clive Tesar

Persistent organic pollutants (POPs) are highly toxic chemicals that have harmful effects on human and wildlife health, argues Clive Tesar in the following viewpoint. Many countries have stopped using the "dirty dozen"—twelve POPs that the United Nations Environment Programme recommends be banned worldwide—but others have not, Tesar maintains. What makes POPs of international concern, he claims, is that they can travel great distances, posing a threat to people living far from the nations that actually use them. Tesar is editor of *Northern Perspectives*, a publication of the Canadian Arctic Resources Committee.

As you read, consider the following questions:

1. In Tesar's opinion, why was DDT used widely during World War II?
2. To what have dioxins been linked, in the author's view?
3. According to the author, how have large numbers of people been exposed to polychlorinated biphenyls (PCBs)?

Clive Tesar, "POPs: What They Are, How They Are Used, How They Are Transported," *Northern Perspectives*, Fall/Winter 2000. Copyright © 2000 by the Canadian Arctic Resources Committee, Inc. Reproduced by permission. To support the Canadian Arctic Resources Committee, visit the online donation form at www.carc.org.

P ersistent organic pollutants (POPs) are carbon-based chemical compounds and mixtures that include industrial chemicals such as PCBs, pesticides like DDT, and unwanted wastes such as dioxins. POPs are primarily products and by-products of human industry that are of relatively recent origin. As the name suggests, they are persistent in the environment, resisting degradation through natural processes.

Of all the pollutants released into the environment every year by human activity, POPs are among the most dangerous. They are highly toxic, causing an array of adverse effects, including disease, birth defects among humans and animals, and death. Specific effects can include cancer, allergies, and hypersensitivity; damage to the central and peripheral nervous systems; reproductive disorders; and disruption of the immune system. Many of these effects are intergenerational, present in both affected adults and their children. A study released in August 2000, *The Health of Canada's Children*, published by the Canadian Institute of Child Health, concludes: "Today's children are born with a body burden of synthetic, persistent organic pollutants—the consequences of which will not be known for another 50 years or so."

A Widespread Problem

Although some countries have already banned the use of some POPs because of their demonstrated toxicity, many are still in use in countries around the globe. Russia, for example, has no plans to phase out its use of PCBs in electrical transformers (a once-common application throughout the developed world) until the useful life of those transformers is over. That could be 2025 or later. There is concern about what will happen if some countries stop using DDT to control malarial mosquitoes. In both cases, wealthier countries must consider assistance to ensure that compliance with a ban on POPs is a reasonable solution. It's a case of enlightened self-interest to do so.

POPs released to the environment can travel through air and water to regions distant from their original source. They travel on wind and water currents, especially through the process of evaporation and redeposition known as the "grasshopper effect." Because Arctic air is cold, evaporation is minimal and POPs tend to accumulate and concentrate in polar regions. For example, levels of lindane, used as a pesticide in China, recorded from the coast of China to the Beaufort Sea show a marked increase near the Arctic. Recent studies have shown high concentrations of POPs are also present in alpine regions.

How long before things improve in the Arctic depends on when these substances are taken out of production. Substances in use today may take several years to reach higher latitudes. Even if all uses of certain POPs were to stop today, experts believe that it would take approximately 50 years for them to disappear from the Arctic.

The Dirty Dozen

Although many POPs exist, the United Nations Environment Programme (UNEP) has targeted the following for immediate action. The description of each chemical and its properties is adapted from information provided by UNEP.

Aldrin—A pesticide applied to soil to kill termites, grasshoppers, corn rootworm, and other insect pests, aldrin can also kill birds, fish, and humans. In one incident, aldrin-treated rice is believed to have killed hundreds of shorebirds, waterfowl, and passerines along the Texas Gulf Coast when these birds ate either the rice or animals that had eaten the rice. In humans, the fatal dose for an adult male is estimated to be about five grams. Humans are exposed to aldrin through dairy products and animal meats. Studies in India indicate that the average daily intake of aldrin and its by-product dieldrin (see below) is about 19 micrograms per person. The use of aldrin has been banned or severely restricted in many countries.

Chlordane—Used extensively to control termites and as a broad-spectrum insecticide on a range of agricultural crops, chlordane remains in the soil for a long time and has a reported half-life of one year. The lethal effects of chlordane on fish and birds vary according to the species, but tests have shown that it can kill mallard ducks, bobwhite quail, and pink shrimp. Chlordane may affect the human immune system and is classified as a possible human carcinogen. It is believed that human exposure occurs mainly through the air, and chlordane has been detected in the indoor air of residences in the United States and Japan. Chlordane is either banned or severely restricted in dozens of countries.

Controlling Pests

DDT—Perhaps the most infamous of the POPs, DDT was widely used during World War II to protect soldiers and civilians from malaria, typhus, and other diseases spread by insects. After the war, DDT continued to be used to control disease, and it was sprayed on a variety of agricultural crops, especially cotton. DDT continues to be applied against mosquitoes in several countries to control malaria. Its stability, its persistence (as much as 50% can remain in the soil 10–15 years after application), and its widespread use have meant that DDT residues can be found everywhere; residual DDT has been detected in the Arctic.

Perhaps the best known toxic effect of DDT is eggshell thinning among birds, especially birds of prey. Its impact on bird populations led to bans in many countries during the 1970s. While 34 countries have banned DDT and 34 others severely restrict its use, it is still detected in food from all over the world. Although residues in domestic animals have declined steadily over the last two decades, food-borne DDT remains the greatest source of exposure for the general population. The short-term acute effects of DDT on humans are limited, but long-term exposures have been associated with chronic health effects. DDT has been detected in breast milk, raising serious concerns about infant health.

Dieldrin—Used principally to control termites and textile pests, dieldrin has also been used to control insect-borne diseases and insects living in agricultural soils. Its half-life in soil is approximately five years. The pesticide aldrin rapidly converts to dieldrin, so concentrations of dieldrin in the environment are higher than dieldrin use alone would indicate. Dieldrin is highly toxic to fish and other aquatic animals, particularly frogs, whose embryos can develop spinal deformities after exposure to low levels. Dieldrin residues have been found in air, water, soil, fish, birds, and mammals, including humans. Food is the primary source of exposure for the general population; dieldrin was the second most common pesticide detected in a U.S. survey of pasteurized milk.

Dioxins—These chemicals are produced unintentionally in incomplete combustion as well as during the manufacture of pesticides and other chlorinated substances. They are emitted mostly in the burning of hospital, municipal, and hazardous wastes, but also when burning peat, coal, and wood and in automobile emissions. Of the 75 different dioxins, seven are considered to be of concern. One type was found to be present in the soil 10–12 years after the first exposure. Dioxins have been linked to a number of adverse effects in humans, including immune and enzyme disorders and chloracne, and they are classified as possible human carcinogens. In laboratory animals dioxins caused a variety of effects, including an increase in birth defects and stillbirths. Fish exposed to dioxins died shortly after the exposure. Food (particularly from animals) is the major source of exposure for humans.

The Products of Agriculture and Industry

Endrin—This insecticide is sprayed on the leaves of crops such as cotton and grains and is also used to control rodents such as mice and voles. Animals can metabolize endrin, so it does not accumulate in their fatty tissue to the extent that structurally similar chemicals do. It has a long half-life, however, persisting in the soil for up to 12 years. In addition, endrin is highly toxic to fish. When exposed to high levels of endrin in the water, sheepshead minnows hatched early and died by the ninth day of their exposure. The primary route of exposure for the general human population is through food, although current dietary intake estimates are below the limits deemed safe by world health authorities.

Furans—These compounds are produced unintentionally from many of the same processes that produce dioxins and during the production of PCBs (see *PCBs*). They have been detected in emissions from waste incinerators and automobiles. Furans are structurally similar to dioxins and share many of their toxic effects. The toxicity of the 135 different types varies. Furans persist in the environment for long periods and are classified as possible human carcinogens. Food, particularly animal products, is the major source of exposure for humans. Furans have been detected in breast-fed infants.

Heptachlor—Primarily used to kill soil insects and termites, heptachlor has also been used to kill cotton insects, grasshoppers, other crop pests, and malaria-carrying mosquitoes. It is believed to be responsible for the decline of several wild-bird populations, including Canadian Geese and American Kestrels in the Columbia River basin in the United States. The geese died after eating seeds treated with levels of heptachlor lower than maximum levels recommended by the manufacturer, suggesting that even responsible use of heptachlor may kill wildlife. Laboratory tests have shown high doses of heptachlor to be fatal to mink, rats, and rabbits, and lower doses to cause adverse behavioural changes and reduced reproductive success. Heptachlor is classified as a possible human carcinogen, and some two dozen countries have either banned it or restricted its use. Food is the major source of exposure for humans, and residues have been detected in the blood of cattle from the United States and Australia.

Gathering Data on POPs

Over the years, environmental scientists have gathered a mountain of evidence that a number of these chemicals—particularly the ones known as persistent organic pollutants (POPs)—cycle the globe, contaminating fields, watersheds, air, and biota. In an increasing number of areas, contaminated sites pose an unknown threat to human health and are endangering clean water resources. At the same time, a growing body of data is linking some of the POPs—including DDT, the first of the chlorinated organic insecticides, and PCBs (polychlorinated biphenyls)—to cancer and various other diseases, and to the disruption of reproductive cycles in humans and animals.

A.J.S. Rayl, *Scientist*, September 2, 2002.

Hexachlorobenzene (HCB)—First introduced in 1945 to treat seeds, HCB kills fungi that affect food crops. It was widely used to control wheat bunt. It is also a by-product of the manufacture of certain industrial chemicals and exists as an impurity in several pesticide formulations. When people in eastern Turkey ate HCB-treated seed grain between 1954 and 1959, they developed a variety of symptoms, including photosensitive skin lesions, colic, and debilitation; of several thousand who developed a metabolic disorder called porphyria turcica, 14% died. Mothers also passed HCB to their infants through the placenta and through breast milk. In high doses, HCB is lethal to some animals, and at lower levels adversely affects their reproductive success. HCB has been found in all food types. A study of Spanish meat found HCB present in all samples. In India, the estimated average daily intake of HCB is 0.13 micrograms per kilogram of body weight.

Mirex—This insecticide is used mainly to combat fire ants, and it has been used against other types of ants and termites. It has also been used as a fire retardant in plastics, rubber, and electrical goods. Direct exposure to mirex does not appear to cause injury to humans, but studies on laboratory animals have caused it to be classified as a possible human carcinogen. In studies, mirex proved toxic to several plant species and to fish and crustaceans. It is considered to be one of the most stable and persistent pesticides, with a half-life as great as 10 years. The main route of human exposure to mirex is through food, particularly meat, fish, and wild game.

Polychlorinated Biphenyls (PCBs)—These compounds are used in industry as heat-exchange fluids in electric transformers and capacitors and as additives in paint, carbonless copy paper, and plastics. Of the 209 different types of PCBs, 13 exhibit a dioxin-like toxicity. Their persistence in the environment corresponds to the degree of chlorination, and half-lives can vary from 10 days to one-and-a-half years. PCBs are toxic to fish, killing them at higher doses and causing spawning failures at lower doses. Research also links PCBs to reproductive failure and suppression of the immune system in various wild animals, such as seals and mink.

Large numbers of people have been exposed to PCBs through food contamination. Consumption of PCB-contaminated rice oil in Japan in 1968 and in Taiwan in 1979 caused pigmentation of nails and mucous membranes and swelling of the eyelids, along with fatigue, nausea, and vomiting. Due to the persistence of PCBs in their mothers' bodies, children born as many as seven years after the Taiwan incident showed developmental delays and behavioural problems. Similarly, children of mothers who ate large amounts of contaminated fish from Lake Michigan showed poorer short-term memory function. PCBs also suppress the human immune system and are listed as probable human carcinogens.

Toxaphene—This insecticide is used on cotton, cereal grains, fruits, nuts, and vegetables. It has also been used to control ticks and mites in livestock. Toxaphene was the most widely used pesticide in the United States in 1975. As much as 50% of a toxaphene release can persist in the soil for as long as 12 years. For humans, the most likely source of toxaphene exposure is food. While the toxicity to humans of direct exposure is not high, toxaphene has been listed as a possible human carcinogen due to its effects on laboratory animals. It is highly toxic to fish; brook trout exposed to toxaphene for 90 days experienced a 46% reduction in weight and reduced egg viability, and long-term exposure to levels of 0.5 micrograms per litre of water reduced egg viability to zero. Thirty-seven countries have banned toxaphene, and 11 others have severely restricted its use.

"The [Persistent Organic Pollutants] treaty is . . . a global death warrant for millions—and, potentially, hundreds of millions—of human beings."

Exaggerated Fears About Persistent Organic Pollutants Threaten World Health

William F. Jasper

Banning persistent organic pollutants (POPs) will not protect human health, contends William F. Jasper in the following viewpoint. In fact, he claims, banning DDT, one of several POPs that policy makers hope to ban, will lead to the death of millions from malaria. DDT, used extensively during and after World War II, effectively reduced malaria for decades, Jasper maintains. Since environmental alarmists convinced world leaders to ban it, however, malaria deaths have increased worldwide. Those behind such bans hope to control world population by allowing malaria to wipe out millions of people, Jasper asserts. Jasper is senior editor of the *New American*.

As you read, consider the following questions:
1. According to the Institute of Medicine, in how many countries is malaria a public health problem?
2. In Dr. Roger Bate's opinion, why did malaria rates around the world decline dramatically after World War II?
3. In Jasper's view, who promotes global enviro-schemes like the POP agreement?

William F. Jasper, "Environmental Genocide," *New American*, vol. 17, July 2, 2001. Copyright © 2004 by American Opinion Publishing Incorporated. Reproduced by permission.

A brutal mass murderer is stalking the planet. Each year he kills millions and leaves millions more injured. Incredibly, while expressing concern over his carnage, the United Nations—with the help of the U.S. government—has given him a free pass to keep up his deadly rampage.

A Murderous Plague

The killer's name is malaria, and the United Nations Convention on Persistent Organic Pollutants (known as the POP Convention) will give this murderous plague permanent protected status. The UN POP Convention, signed by representatives of more than 100 nations in Stockholm on May 23, [2001] is heralded by the radical eco-lobby and the media as a tremendous boon for humankind and the planet. Yet, the POP treaty is, in truth, a global death warrant for millions—and, potentially, hundreds of millions—of human beings.

"Malaria, which had been eliminated or effectively suppressed in many parts of the world, is undergoing a resurgence," warned the Institute of Medicine of the National Academy of Sciences in 1996. "It is a public health problem today in more than 90 countries inhabited by some 2,400 million people—40 percent of the world's population. Malaria is estimated to cause up to 500 million clinical cases and 2.7 million deaths each year. Every 30 seconds, a child somewhere dies of malaria. The global effects of the disease threaten public health and productivity on a broad scale and impede the progress of many countries toward democracy and prosperity."

"The human dimensions of malaria are staggering. It is, by far, the most devastating and deadly parasitic disease in the world," notes the Malaria Foundation International (MFI), one of the world's leading anti-malaria organizations. Or as Dr. Wenceslaus Kilama, chairman of MFI, has stated, the current malaria epidemic "is like loading up seven Boeing 747 airliners each day, then deliberately crashing them into Mt. Kilimanjaro."

Unnecessary Deaths

The most staggering aspect of malaria's horrendous death toll, however, is the fact that most of these deaths are unnecessary. Millions of lives could be saved and the suffering of hundreds of millions prevented for a relatively small cost—and with "old" technology. That technology is DDT (dichlorodiphenyltrichlorethane), a pesticide that has proven to be a veritable godsend to mankind, even as it has been subjected to a campaign of vilification over the past four decades.

Dr. Roger Bate, a director of Africa Fighting Malaria, a South African non-governmental organization, reminds us that the heroic malaria-eradication program following World War II used DDT as its primary weapon. "This program succeeded in North America and southern Europe, and greatly reduced incidence in many other countries," says Dr. Bate. "Spraying DDT in houses and on mosquito breeding grounds was the primary reason that rates of malaria around the world declined dramatically after the Second World War," Dr. Bate notes in his study, *When Politics Kills: Malaria and the DDT Story*, published by the Competitive Enterprise Institute. "Nearly one million Indians died from malaria in 1945, but DDT spraying reduced this to a few thousand by 1960. However, concerns about the environmental harm of DDT led to a decline in spraying, and likewise, a resurgence of malaria. Today there are once again millions of cases of malaria in India, and over 300 million cases worldwide—most in sub-Saharan Africa. Cases of malaria in South Africa have risen by over 1000 percent in the past five years. Only those countries that have continued to use DDT, such as Ecuador, have contained or reduced malaria."

The MFI reports that due to Sri Lanka's use of DDT in a mosquito abatement program, "in only 8 years, Sri Lanka went from a million cases of malaria a year to only seventeen." When the DDT spraying was stopped, however, "malaria rebounded to nearly a million cases a year" within a decade.

The Impact in Africa

Dr. Bate records similar results in Africa:

> Not long after DDT was removed from malaria control in South Africa in 1996, disease rates rocketed, particularly in northern KwaZulu Natal. A serious problem was that Anopheles funestus mosquitoes developed resistance to synthetic pyrethroids—the main alternative to DDT—making

the switch an expensive and futile exercise. According to Rajendra Maharaj, head of vector control at the South African department of health, it is unlikely that [Anopheles] funestus would ever have returned had DDT remained in use.

One need only compare malaria rates in South Africa, Swaziland and Mozambique to see the effect of banning DDT. Swaziland never halted DDT spraying and infection rates range between 2 and 4 per cent. A short distance over the border in South Africa, infection rates average about 40 per cent. In Mozambique, infection rates are over 80 per cent, owing in part to the collapse of the malaria control program during that country's war. . . . DDT is now back in use in KwaZulu Natal and according to Jotham Mthembu, head of the malaria control program at Jozini in KZN, conditions have improved.

DDT was developed by Dr. Paul Müller, a Swiss chemist who received the Nobel Prize in Medicine in 1948, in recognition of the enormous medical importance of this remarkable chemical substance. Though widely used for only three decades, DDT has been justifiably credited with preventing more human deaths by disease than any chemical ever concocted.

Yet, the government of the United States has joined forces with environmental organizations and the United Nations to deny this important life-saving tool to those who most desperately need it. The UN POP Convention has targeted 12 chemicals that it has dubbed "The Dirty Dozen" for elimination or severe restriction. While not scheduled for outright elimination (at least not yet), the POP restrictions on DDT will render it too costly and inaccessible to those countries in most serious need.

Backing from Bush

If a Clinton or Gore administration had announced its intent to sign the POP Convention, one could be sure of an avalanche of furious denunciations from the loyal opposition. GOP congressmen and conservative commentators would have scorched the Oval Office for "green extremism" and environmental genocide. Al Gore's embarrassingly ridiculous 1992 ecological manifesto, *Earth in the Balance*, would have been dredged up once more for rhetorical target practice.

Nevertheless, while the presidential remarks emanating from the White House Rose Garden on April 19 [2001] sounded like a rip-and-read from Gore's infamous book, the words were coming out of the mouth of George W. Bush. Flanked by [former] Secretary of State Colin Powell and [former] EPA Administrator Christine Todd Whitman, to underscore the importance of his announcement, President Bush proclaimed: "Negotiations were begun by the previous administration, and this treaty achieves a goal shared by this administration. I am pleased to announce my support for the [POP] treaty and the intention of our government to sign and submit it for approval by the United States Senate."

Controlling Disease with DDT

The green movement's attitude to DDT in disease control was, and is, nothing short of callous and couched in a neo-Malthusian idea that global populations are growing out of control and that resources are running out. Malaria is, therefore, perversely seen as a saving grace from impending environmental disaster.

Critically, the EPA [Environmental Protection Agency] did not sufficiently point out that the dose of DDT used in vector [disease-carrying organism] control is tiny compared with the amount that was being used in agriculture. And the dose of DDT received is vital for any harm to occur. There simply is no danger to the environment or human beings from using DDT in vector control, even if there was from agricultural use.

Roger Bate, Pacific Research Institute speech, September 25, 2001.

Adopting the vernacular of the radical environmentalists at Greenpeace and the Environmental Defense Fund, President Bush declared that "this international agreement would restrict the use of 12 dangerous chemicals—POPs, as they are known, or the Dirty Dozen."

The Republican president went on to proclaim that "concerns over the hazards of PCBs, DDT, and the other toxic chemicals covered by the agreement are based on solid scientific information. These pollutants are linked to developmental defects, cancer, and other grave problems in humans and animals. The risks are great, and the need for action is clear. We must work to eliminate, or at least to severely restrict the release of these toxins without delay."

Citing the POP treaty as a wondrous "bipartisan" victory, Bush announced that "now a Republican administration will continue and complete the work of a Democratic administration. This is the way environmental policy should work."

Unfortunately, this is the way environmental policy *does* work amongst our bipartisan globalists in Washington. This seeming Republican reversal on the POP treaty should not have surprised anyone. As James M. Lindsay of the Brookings Institution pointed out . . . during the closing weeks of the [2000] Bush-Gore election race, "both Al Gore and George W. Bush are internationalists by inclination. . . ."

The Drive for Depopulation

Given the life-and-death stakes involved in the DDT-malaria conflict, questions naturally arise: Don't the POP champions realize the deadly consequences of their actions? Don't they know that millions of people will die as a result of enforcement of the POP restrictions? Obviously, many of the pedestrian-level "environmentalists" do not; many of these well-meaning do-gooders would be shocked if the real nature and effects of this treaty were explained to them. However, the CFR [Council on Foreign Relations] insiders who spawn and promote these global enviro-schemes know full well the lethal measure of their proposals. These organized globalists have been fully apprised by eminent scientists and learned societies of the terrible cost in lives, suffering, and dollars that will result from their policies, and they have proceeded apace nonetheless. They know that President Bush's claim that the POP agreement is "based on solid scientific information" is ludicrous; they know it is based on junk science and deadly deception.

What's more, we can logically surmise that many of these one-world elitists are culpable of actually intending the terrible outcome that enforcement of the POP treaty will surely bring: the condemnation of fellow human beings to death by depriving them of the readily available means of protecting themselves. We can make this surmise because they have told us so in their own self-indicting speeches and writings.

During the debates over DDT in the late 1960s, Dr. Charles Wurster, chief scientist for the radical Environmental Defense Fund (EDF), responded to a reporter's question about DDT's life-saving potential by saying there are too many people on the planet already. Banning DDT, he said, "is as good a way to get rid of them as any." "Them" refers to all of the millions of hapless victims—primarily in developing countries—whom people like Wurster view as excess baggage. "Them" includes "all those little brown people in poor countries," as fellow depopulationist Dr. Van den Bosch of the University of California so indelicately phrased it.

But it's not only Third World "brown people" who are targeted for elimination. During a 1971 House Committee on Agriculture hearing on DDT, Representative John Rarick revealed this quote by Dr. Wurster, whose EDF has been lavishly funded for decades by the CFR-dominated tax exempt foundations: "It really doesn't make a lot of difference because the organophosphate [pesticide] acts locally and only kills farm workers, and most of them are Mexicans and Negroes."

Targeting the Human Species

If you do not fit that racial profile, don't imagine that you have been neglected by the one-world eugenicists. Friends of the Earth founder David Brower, another radical environmentalist long favored by the CFR Establishment, has targeted you too. In his *Earth Day—The Beginning*, a "survival guide" published in 1970, Brower declared: "That's the first thing to do—start controlling the population in affluent white America, where a child born to a white American will use about fifty times the resources of a child born in the black ghetto." Brower also proclaimed: "Childbearing [should be] a punishable crime against society, unless the parents hold a government license. . . . All potential parents [should be] required to use contraceptive chemicals, the government issuing antidotes to citizens chosen for childbearing."

One of the most chilling admissions of deadly intent came from the lips of the late Jacques Cousteau, the sainted environmental icon. In an interview with the *UNESCO Courier* for November 1991 the famed oceanographer said:

The damage people cause to the planet is a function of demographics—it is equal to the degree of development. One American burdens the earth much more than twenty Bangaladeshes. The damage is directly linked to consumption. Our society is turning toward more and needless consumption. It is a vicious circle that I compare to cancer. . . .

This is a terrible thing to say. In order to stabilize world population, we must eliminate 350,000 people per day. It is a horrible thing to say, but it's just as bad not to say it.

Later, just before the Earth Summit, Cousteau told Jean Daniel, senior editor of the French weekly *Nouvelle Observateur:* "More and more people are willing to use the atomic bomb if the situation arises that one billion people are migrating toward the West." Cousteau didn't explicitly say that *he* would be willing to use the bomb, but the inference was that such drastic measures may be not only justified, but possibly essential, to attain "sustainable" world population levels. . . .

The POP Convention is merely an opening round in the UN's war against that great "enemy," humanity. Even malaria will not be sufficiently lethal to satisfy the depopulation goals of the globalists.

"Worldwide, more than one billion people presently lack access to clean water sources."

Water Pollution Poses a Serious Threat

Joseph Orlins and Anne Wehrly

Water pollution remains a serious threat to human health and the environment, assert Joseph Orlins and Anne Wehrly in the following viewpoint. The U.S. government regulates water pollution from identifiable "point" sources, but pollution from "nonpoint" sources (the source cannot be identified) continues to pollute America's waters, the authors maintain. Dangerous pollutants enter waters near urban areas when rain carries contaminated runoff from streets into storm drains. Pollutants also flow into bodies of water when irrigation washes toxic fertilizer and pesticides from farms and lawns into streams. Orlins is a civil engineering professor at Rowan University in Glassboro, New Jersey; Wehrly is a freelance writer and attorney.

As you read, consider the following questions:

1. According to Orlins and Wehrly, what forms can water pollutants take?
2. What are some examples of point sources, in the authors' view?
3. In the authors' opinion, what are some of the adverse effects water pollution has on ecosystems?

Joseph Orlins and Anne Wehrly, "The Quest for Clean Water," *World & I*, vol. 18, May 2003. Copyright © 2003 by News World Communications, Inc. Reproduced by permission.

In the 1890s, entrepreneur William Love sought to establish a model industrial community in the La Salle district of Niagara Falls, New York. The plan included building a canal that tapped water from the Niagara River for a navigable waterway and a hydroelectric power plant. Although work on the canal was begun, a nationwide economic depression and other factors forced abandonment of the project.

The Tragedy of Love Canal

By 1920, the land adjacent to the canal was sold and used as a landfill for municipal and industrial wastes. Later purchased by Hooker Chemicals and Plastics Corp., the landfill became a dumping ground for nearly 21,000 tons of mixed chemical wastes before being closed and covered over in the early 1950s. Shortly thereafter, the property was acquired by the Niagara Falls Board of Education, and schools and residences were built on and around the site.

In the ensuing decades, groundwater levels in the area rose, parts of the landfill subsided, large metal drums of waste were uncovered, and toxic chemicals oozed out. All this led to the contamination of surface waters, oily residues in residential basements, corrosion of sump pumps, and noxious odors. Residents began to question if these problems were at the root of an apparent prevalence of birth defects and miscarriages in the neighborhood.

Eventually, in 1978, the area was declared unsafe by the New York State Department of Health, and President Jimmy Carter approved emergency federal assistance. The school located on the landfill site was closed and nearby houses were condemned. State and federal agencies worked together to relocate hundreds of residents and contain or destroy the chemical wastes.

That was the bitter story of Love Canal. Although not the worst environmental disaster in U.S. history, it illustrates the tragic consequences of water pollution.

Water Quality Standards

In addition to toxic chemical wastes, water pollutants occur in many other forms, including pathogenic microbes (harmful bacteria and viruses), excess fertilizers (containing compounds of phosphorus and nitrogen), and trash floating on streams, lakes, and beaches. Water pollution can also take the form of sediment eroded from stream banks, large blooms of algae, low levels of dissolved oxygen, or abnormally high temperatures (from the discharge of coolant water at power plants).

The United States has seen a growing concern about water pollution since the middle of the twentieth century, as the public recognized that pollutants were adversely affecting human health and rendering lakes unswimmable, streams unfishable, and rivers flammable. In response, in 1972, Congress passed the Federal Water Pollution Control Act Amendments, later modified and referred to as the Clean Water Act. Its purpose was to "restore and maintain the chemical, physical, and biological integrity of the nation's waters."

The Clean Water Act set the ambitious national goal of completely eliminating the discharge of pollutants into navigable waters by 1985, as well as the interim goal of making water clean enough to sustain fish and wildlife, while being safe for swimming and boating. To achieve these goals, certain standards for water quality were established.

The "designated uses" of every body of water subject to the act must first be identified. Is it a source for drinking water? Is it used for recreation, such as swimming? Does it supply agriculture or industry? Is it a significant habitat for fish and other aquatic life? Thereafter, the water must be tested for pollutants. If it fails to meet the minimum standards for its designated uses, then steps must be taken to limit pollutants entering it, so that it becomes suitable for those uses.

On the global level, the fundamental importance of clean water has come into the spotlight. In November 2002, the UN [United Nations] Committee on Economic, Cultural and Social Rights declared access to clean water a human right. Moreover, the United Nations has designated 2003 to be the International Year of Freshwater, with the aim of encouraging sustainable use of freshwater and integrated water resources management.

Here, There, and Everywhere

Implementing the Clean Water Act requires clarifying the sources of pollutants. They are divided into two groups:

"point sources" and "nonpoint sources." Point sources correspond to discrete, identifiable locations from which pollutants are emitted. They include factories, wastewater treatment plants, landfills, and underground storage tanks. Water pollution that originates at point sources is usually what is associated with headline-grabbing stories such as those about Love Canal.

Nonpoint sources of pollution are diffuse and therefore harder to control. For instance, rain washes oil, grease, and solid pollutants from streets and parking lots into storm drains that carry them into bays and rivers. Likewise, irrigation and rainwater leach fertilizers, herbicides, and insecticides from farms and lawns and into streams and lakes.

The direct discharge of wastes from point sources into lakes, rivers, and streams is regulated by a permit program known as the National Pollutant Discharge Elimination System (NPDES). This program, established through the Clean Water Act, is administered by the Environmental Protection Agency (EPA) and authorized states. By regulating the wastes discharged, NPDES has helped reduce point-source pollution dramatically. On the other hand, water pollution in the United States is now mainly from nonpoint sources, as reported by the EPA.

Studying Watersheds

In 1991, the U.S. Geological Survey (USGS, part of the Department of the Interior) began a systematic, long-term program to monitor watersheds. The National Water-Quality Assessment Program (NAWQA), established to help manage surface and groundwater supplies, has involved the collection and analysis of water quality data in over 50 major river basins and aquifer systems in nearly all 50 states.

The program has encompassed three principal categories of investigation: (1) the current conditions of surface water and groundwater; (2) changes in those conditions over time; and (3) major factors—such as climate, geography, and land use—that affect water quality. For each of these categories, the water and sediment have been tested for such pollutants as pesticides, plant nutrients, volatile organic compounds, and heavy metals.

The NAWQA findings were disturbing. Water quality is most affected in watersheds with highest population density and urban development. In agricultural areas, 95 percent of tested streams and 60 percent of shallow wells contained herbicides, insecticides, or both. In urban areas, 99 percent of tested streams and 50 percent of shallow wells had herbicides, especially those used on lawns and golf courses. Insec-

How Urban Areas Affect Runoff

Increased Runoff. The porous and varied terrain of natural landscapes like forests, wetlands, and grasslands trap rainwater and snowmelt and allow it to slowly filter into the ground. Runoff tends to reach receiving waters gradually. In contrast, nonporous urban landscapes like roads, bridges, parking lots, and buildings don't let runoff slowly percolate into the ground. Water remains above the surface, accumulates, and runs off in large amounts.

Cities install storm sewer systems that quickly channel this runoff from roads and other impervious surfaces. Runoff gathers speed once it enters the storm sewer system. When it leaves the system and empties into a stream, large volumes of quickly flowing runoff erode streambanks, damage streamside vegetation, and widen stream channels. In turn, this will result in lower water depths during non-storm periods, higher than normal water levels during wet weather periods, increased sediment loads, and higher water temperatures. Native fish and other aquatic life cannot survive in urban streams severely impacted by urban runoff.

Increased Pollutant Loads. Urbanization also increases the variety and amount of pollutants transported to receiving waters. Sediment from development and new construction; oil, grease, and toxic chemicals from automobiles; nutrients and pesticides from turf management and gardening; viruses and bacteria from failing septic systems; road salts; and heavy metals are examples of pollutants generated in urban areas. Sediments and solids constitute the largest volume of pollutant loads to receiving waters in urban areas.

When runoff enters storm drains, it carries many of these pollutants with it. In older cities, this polluted runoff is often released directly into the water without any treatment. Increased pollutant loads can harm fish and wildlife populations, kill native vegetation, foul drinking water supplies, and make recreational areas unsafe.

U.S. Environmental Protection Agency, "Nonpoint Source Pointers," 2003.

ticides were found more frequently in urban streams than in agricultural ones.

The study also found large amounts of plant nutrients in water supplies. For instance, 80 percent of agricultural streams and 70 percent of urban streams were found to contain phosphorus at concentrations that exceeded EPA guidelines.

Moreover, in agricultural areas, one out of five well-water samples had nitrate concentrations higher than EPA standards for drinking water. Nitrate contamination can result from nitrogen fertilizers or material from defective septic systems leaching into the groundwater, or it may reflect defects in the wells.

The Effects of Pollution

According to the UN World Water Assessment Programme, about 2.3 billion people suffer from diseases associated with polluted water, and more than 5 million people die from these illnesses each year. Dysentery, typhoid, cholera, and hepatitis A are some of the ailments that result from ingesting water contaminated with harmful microbes. Other illnesses—such as malaria, filariasis, yellow fever, and sleeping sickness—are transmitted by vector organisms (such as mosquitoes and tsetse flies) that breed in or live near stagnant, unclean water.

A number of chemical contaminants—including DDT, dioxins, polychlorinated biphenyls (PCBs), and heavy metals—are associated with conditions ranging from skin rashes to various cancers and birth defects. Excess nitrate in an infant's drinking water can lead to the "blue baby syndrome" (methemoglobinemia)—a condition in which the child's digestive system cannot process the nitrate, diminishing the blood's ability to carry adequate concentrations of oxygen.

Besides affecting human health, water pollution has adverse effects on ecosystems. For instance, while moderate amounts of nutrients in surface water are generally not problematic, large quantities of phosphorus and nitrogen compounds can lead to excessive growth of algae and other nuisance species. Known as eutrophication, this phenomenon reduces the penetration of sunlight through the water; when the plants die and decompose, the body of water is left with odors, bad taste, and reduced levels of dissolved oxygen.

Low levels of dissolved oxygen can kill fish and shellfish. In addition, aquatic weeds can interfere with recreational activities (such as boating and swimming) and can clog intake by industry and municipal systems.

Some pollutants settle to the bottom of streams, lakes, and harbors, where they may remain for many years. For instance, although DDT and PCBs were banned years ago, they are still found in sediments in many urban and rural streams. They occur at levels harmful to wildlife at more than two-thirds of the urban sites tested.

Prevention and Remediation

As the old saying goes, an ounce of prevention is worth a pound of cure. This is especially true when it comes to controlling water pollution. Several important steps taken since the passage of the Clean Water Act have made surface waters today cleaner in many ways than they were 30 years ago.

For example, industrial wastes are mandated to be neutralized or broken down before being discharged to streams, lakes, and harbors. Moreover, the U.S. government has banned the production and use of certain dangerous pollutants such as DDT and PCBs.

In addition, two major changes have been introduced in the handling of sewage. First, smaller, less efficient sewage treatment plants are being replaced with modern, regional plants that include biological treatment, in which microorganisms are used to break down organic matter in the sewage. The newer plants are releasing much cleaner discharges into the receiving bodies of water (rivers, lakes, and ocean).

Second, many jurisdictions throughout the United States are building separate sewer lines for storm water and sanitary wastes. These upgrades are needed because excess water in the older, "combined" sewer systems would simply bypass the treatment process, and untreated sewage would be discharged directly into receiving bodies of water.

Minimizing Nonpoint Sources

To minimize pollutants from nonpoint sources, the EPA is requiring all municipalities to address the problem of runoff from roads and parking lots. At the same time, the use of fertilizers and pesticides needs to be reduced. Toward this end, county extension agents are educating farmers and homeowners about their proper application and the availability of nutrient testing.

To curtail the use of expensive and potentially harmful pesticides, the approach known as integrated pest management can be implemented. It involves the identification of specific pest problems and the use of nontoxic chemicals and chemical-free alternatives whenever possible. For instance, aphids can be held in check by ladybug beetles and caterpillars can be controlled by applying neem oil to the leaves on which they feed.

Moreover, new urban development projects in many areas are required to implement storm-water management practices. They include such features as: oil and grease traps in storm drains; swales to slow down runoff, allowing it to infiltrate back into groundwater; "wet" detention basins (essentially artificial ponds) that allow solids to settle out of runoff; and artificial wetlands that help break down contaminants in runoff. While such additions may be costly, they significantly improve water quality. They are of course much more expensive to install after those areas have been developed.

Once a waterway is polluted, cleanup is often expensive and time consuming. For instance, to increase the concentration of dissolved oxygen in a lake that has undergone eutrophication, fountains and aerators may be necessary. Specially designed boats may be needed to harvest nuisance weeds.

At times, it is costly just to identify the source of a problem. For example, if a body of water contains high levels of coliform bacteria, expensive DNA testing may be needed to determine whether the bacteria came from leakage of human sewage, pet waste, or the feces of waterfowl or other wildlife.

Contaminated sediments are sometimes difficult to treat. Available techniques range from dredging the sediments to "capping" them in place, to limit their potential exposure. Given that they act as reservoirs of pollutants, it is often best to remove the sediments and burn off the contaminants. Alternatively, the extracted sediments may be placed in confined disposal areas that prevent the pollutants from leaching back into groundwater. Dredging, however, may create additional problems by releasing pollutants back into the water column when the sediment is stirred up.

The Future of Clean Water

The EPA reports that as a result of the Clean Water Act, millions of tons of sewage and industrial waste are being treated before they are discharged into U.S. coastal waters. In addition, the majority of lakes and rivers now meet mandated water quality goals.

Yet the future of federal regulation under the Clean Water Act is unclear. In 2001, a Supreme Court decision (*Solid Waste Agency of Northern Cook County v. United States Army Corps of Engineers, et al.*) brought into question the power of federal agencies to regulate activities affecting water quality in smaller, nonnavigable bodies of water. This and related court decisions have set the stage for the EPA and other federal agencies to redefine which bodies of water can be protected from unregulated dumping and discharges under the Clean Water Act. As a result, individual states may soon be faced with much greater responsibility for the protection of water resources.

Worldwide, more than one billion people presently lack access to clean water sources, and over two billion live without basic sanitation facilities. A large proportion of those who die from water-related diseases are infants. We would hope that by raising awareness of these issues on an international level, the newly recognized right to clean water will become a reality for a much larger percentage of the world's population.

"*The proliferation of artificial lighting threatens wildlife, ruins habitat, fouls the air, squanders resources, and blocks our view of the heavens.*"

Light Pollution Is a Serious Problem

Joe Bower

Light pollution is a serious problem that threatens the environment, claims Joe Bower in the following viewpoint. Light pollution not only makes it more difficult for people to see the stars, but some animals become confused by the increasing use of artificial light, he maintains. Migrating birds that travel at night, for example, lose their way in artificial light; as a result, nearly 100 million birds are killed each year, Bower asserts. In addition, the fuel needed to generate electricity contributes to smog, acid rain, and greenhouse gases, he argues. Bower writes on environmental issues for publications such as *Audubon* and *National Wildlife*.

As you read, consider the following questions:
1. In Bower's opinion, how many Americans live in areas where they can see stars that should be visible under normal nighttime conditions?
2. According to the author, what has happened to the hatchlings of sea turtles in Florida?
3. How does the author explain the push toward overlighting?

Joe Bower, "The Dark Side of Light," *Audubon*, vol. 102, March 2000, p. 92.

L as Vegas it's not. But the small city I live in, Kalamazoo, Michigan, still puts on quite a light show. As night falls, thousands of lamps flicker, blink, pulsate, and shine. Incandescent, fluorescent, mercury-vapor, metal halide, and halogen. White, red, blue, yellow, orange. We've got them all here in Kalamazoo. You should see them from the hill near my house. It's a sight, especially during the holidays. But if you're ever admiring the spectacle, I hope you appreciate the costs involved in staging it. Leaving the lights on is more expensive than you'd think. It not only costs a chunk of change, but it also takes a surprising toll on the environment. The proliferation of artificial lighting threatens wildlife, ruins habitat, fouls the air, squanders resources, and blocks our view of the heavens. No wonder the pervasive problem has come to be called light pollution.

Blocking the Visibility of Stars

Astronomers were the first to notice this problem. About 30 years ago they began to be frustrated as sky glow, the eerie radiance that emanates from settled areas and has spread with urban sprawl, began impairing their ability to see the stars.

Today as few as one in 10 Americans live in areas where they can see the 2,500 or so stars that should be visible under normal nighttime conditions. In most big cities, you're lucky to glimpse a few dozen—on a good night. But light pollution isn't just an urban problem. In Springfield, Vermont, a controversy has erupted over the economically depressed town's decision to permit the construction of a prison; the lights from the site, it is feared, would mar the view from Breezy Hill, one of New England's best places for stargazing. Each year since 1926, thousands have flocked to Breezy Hill for a celebration of the stars called Stellafane. David Levy, an astronomer, has led the protest against the proposed prison. "Stellafane is a magical place, a sanctuary to the stars," he wrote in *Sky & Telescope* magazine.

The Impact on Migrating Birds

Although light pollution's impact on stargazing is as clear as day, its effects on other environmental elements are just coming into focus. The evidence shows that artificial lighting has dire consequences for animal behavior, particularly on the ability to navigate at night.

The hundreds of species of migrating birds that fly after the sun sets, including most songbirds and many shorebirds, are prime examples. Normally they rely on constellations to guide them during their twice-yearly migrations. But scientists speculate that when they fly near urban areas, the bright lights short-circuit their steering sense. Numerous reports have documented birds flying off course toward lights on buildings, towers, lighthouses, even boats. "Both birds and insects demonstrate positive phototaxis," says Sidney Gauthreaux, a Clemson University biologist. "To put it simply, birds are attracted to light much like moths are to a flame. But the reasons are unclear. They may use it as a reference and home in on it." When birds suddenly reach the light's source, they often seem to become confused or blinded by the glare, which can be disastrous.

Birds may slam into windows, walls, floodlights, or even the ground. On the night of October 7, 1954, for instance, 50,000 birds were killed when they followed the beam of a guide light at Warner Robins Air Force Base in Georgia—straight into the ground. The problem is particularly acute when the weather is bad. On a rainy, foggy Labor Day weekend in 1981, more than 10,000 birds collided with the flood-lit smokestacks at Ontario's Hydro Lennox Generating Station, near Kingston. And on January 22, 1998, between 5,000 and 10,000 Lapland longspurs crashed into radio transmission towers near Syracuse, Kansas.

Birds that are distracted by tower lights also may end up crashing into one another. "Around communication towers with constant lights, birds curve, circle, pause, and hover around the lights," Gauthreaux explains. They are apparently trying to orient their flight to the light, which they mistake for the moon or a star. "Over time there's a buildup of migrants [all trying to adjust their course], raising the possibility of hitting guylines or other birds."

Nobody is certain of the total number killed across North America. But Michael Mesure of the Fatal Light Awareness Program (FLAP), a Toronto organization working to publicize the problem, estimates that at least 100 million birds are killed annually by manmade structures. "More birds die each year through collisions than died in the *Exxon Valdez* spill," he says. A tall building in the path of a migration can claim hundreds of lives. One example: From 1982 to 1996, 1,500 migrating birds have smacked into Chicago's McCormick Place Exposition Center.

Although few nocturnal migrants seem immune to light's dark side—for example, dead or injured members of 141 different bird species have been found at McCormick Place—songbirds may be most at risk, Mesure says, because they fly at low altitudes dominated by artificial light.

Passerines are not the only order of birds waylaid by lights. The Newell's shearwater, an endangered Hawaiian seabird, is particularly vulnerable. After their parents abandon their cliffside nests in October and November, fledglings make their first flights by relying on their innate attraction to light to guide them. Normally, because of the light's reflection on water, they fly out to sea, toward the horizon. But when the moon is neither full nor visible, many of the shearwaters instead glide toward lights in seaside resorts and towns. Disoriented, hundreds crash into structures or drop from the sky. In 1998 volunteers gathered 819 shearwaters on the island of Kauai. Most were exhausted or injured, though fortunately, only 77 died.

The Threat to Other Animals

Other animals are threatened by light pollution, too. Hatchlings of at least five sea-turtle species found in Florida rely on an instinctive attraction to light to guide them to water. But lights on or near the beach can confuse the turtles and cause them to head in the wrong direction. Scientists have seen hatchlings cross parking lots, streets, and yards—transfixed by shining streetlights or porch lights. "Their reliance on light is so strong that they'll continue heading to a light source, even if it's an abandoned fire that burns them alive," says Blair Witherington, a Florida Marine Research Institute scientist who studies sea turtles. Disoriented hatchlings usually die from exhaustion, dehydration, or predation. Many others are squashed by cars.

Insects cannot seem to resist this fatal attraction either.

Most people know that moths find lights irresistible. But what they may not realize is that the energy moths expend in this way can cost females the chance to attract a mate. What's more, it can interfere with locating prime spots to lay their eggs, thus giving larvae inadequate conditions to develop, according to Michael Collins, a lepidopterist at the Carnegie Museum. Some entomologists speculate that the proliferation of outdoor lights has contributed to the decline of numerous satumiid moth species in the northeastern United States.

A Lost Heritage

During this century, most people have lost the spectacular view of the universe that their ancestors enjoyed on clear nights. The development of electrical lighting technology and the increase in urban population have caused a rapid increase in sky glow above towns and cities. Few members of the general public have ever seen a prime dark sky. For urban dwellers, star-studded nights are limited to simulations at planetaria. Comets Hyakutake and Hale-Bopp, the most spectacular comets of our time, were for many people merely dim fuzz-balls because of the glare of light pollution.

David L. Crawford, International Dark-Sky Association, 1999.

Visual orientation is just one sense disrupted by artificial light, though it probably isn't the only one, says Meredith West, an Indiana University professor specializing in avian development. Studies of animals raised in controlled settings, like laboratories and poultry farms, indicate that lighting can affect certain "photo-periodic" behavior, including foraging and reproduction. "Animals are very sensitive to light," West says. "Lighting is a powerful stimulus on behavior. If there's enough of it, it can make them act in ways they wouldn't normally." If enough light is present—say, in a well-lit neighborhood—it's possible that animals living there would be stimulated to act as they do during longer days. Overexposure to light may explain reports from English researchers about robins singing at night if there are streetlights in their territories, or why some birds build nests during the fall, instead of spring: Their internal clocks have gone haywire.

Adult female sea turtles will not emerge from the water to nest and lay eggs on beaches that are bathed in artificial light. Many behaviors influenced by changing light—from night to day and the seasonal increases of longer days—involve hormones. "Anything that alters the hormonal system will bring enormous changes," West says. "Hormones regulate growth and immune functions. But they're not produced all the time. If they don't shut down, you overload the body. It can't get rid of them. Hormones are toxic in the wrong amounts." Indeed, a 1998 study at the Mary Imogene Bassett Research Institute in Cooperstown, New York, found that cancerous liver cells in lab rats grew rapidly when they were constantly exposed to light.

The Problem with Burning Coal

Even if wildlife were able to ignore direct sources of light, lighting's impact on the environment would still be unavoidable. Burning coal and oil, according to the Environmental Protection Agency, generates most of the electricity for lights. The process is a dirty one that each year spews out billions of tons of carbon dioxide (CO_2), a greenhouse gas; sulfur dioxide (SO_2), an ingredient of acid rain; and nitrogen oxides (NO_x), which cause smog. Sadly, much of this atmospheric pollution is produced for nothing. "One-third of our lighting is wasted because it shines upward or sideways, illuminating nothing but the bottoms of birds and airplanes," says David L. Crawford of the International Dark-Sky Association (IDA), a 10-year-old anti-light-pollution group based in Tucson. Every year this waste squanders the equivalent of 8.2 million tons of coal or 30 million barrels of oil.

How did we reach this point? A big reason is a push toward overlighting. "People think brighter is better," says Crawford. To lure customers, retailers plug in bigger, brighter signs and entrance lights. In commercial buildings, more electricity is now used for lighting than anything else, even computers or air-conditioning. Urban sprawl has increased the number of lights on streets, billboards, and buildings. Meanwhile, homes are getting bigger and using more electricity. The average single-family home currently consumes 1,500 kilowatt-hours a year for lighting—40 percent more than it did in 1970. To produce that much electricity, power plants emit more than a ton of CO_2, 13 pounds of SO_2, and 8 pounds of NO_x. "Most people are in the dark about lights," Crawford says. "There's a total lack of awareness" of the consequences of lighting.

Of course, using less energy would reduce emissions. In addition, research in Toronto and Washington, D.C. shows that when building lights are dimmed or turned off, the number of fatally attracted birds drops dramatically. "If you have a tower without lights, you'll cause bird collisions, but at least you won't be attracting more birds to it," Gauthreaux says.

Educating the Public

The challenge for the government and environmental groups is to, no pun intended, enlighten people. The Environmental Protection Agency has created an energy-saving program, Energy Star, to help companies and residents reduce lighting use. Several manufacturers have begun producing energy-efficient lights and appliances. FLAP launched a 12-step bird-friendly program that encourages buildings to turn down lights during migrations; it has been adopted at 100 buildings in downtown Toronto since 1997. FLAP organizers are leading similar efforts to raise awareness in Chicago and New York. And educational drives to publicize the impact of light on turtle hatchlings and seabird fledglings are now being sponsored by the National Park Service in Hawaii and by county governments in Florida. Some cities, including Tucson and Miami, are replacing inefficient streetlights with ones designed to focus the beam more sharply. In addition, last August [1999] two workshops at the American Ornithologists' Union conference explored light pollution's impact on birds.

Meanwhile, lawmakers in hundreds of communities have passed ordinances that restrict lighting types, power, and use. Last spring Texas and New Mexico became the fourth and fifth states (along with Arizona, Connecticut, and Maine) to implement a statewide light-restriction program. The ordinances vary in scope, from banning certain types of streetlights or limiting their wattage to shielding security lights. Similar actions are being considered in other states.

Any dark-sky proponent will admit that the national impact of these programs is minimal. But Crawford of the International Dark-Sky Association believes that they're a good start. "I liken lighting to smoking," he says. "All the evidence shows it's bad. But we have to educate people about the consequences. Smoking bans are coming quickly now. But the education that brought them about took a long time."

Periodical Bibliography

The following articles have been selected to supplement the diverse views presented in this chapter.

Hajime Akimoto   "Global Air Quality and Pollution," *Science*, December 5, 2003.

Daniel K. Benjamin   "The Benefits of Clean Air," *PERC Reports*, March 2004.

Paul Burka   "Clearing the Air," *Texas Monthly*, December 2000.

Mitchell Cohen and Brooklyn Greens   "Toxic Wastes and the New World Order," *Synthesis/Regeneration*, Fall 2000.

Christopher D. Cook   "Environmental Hogwash: The EPA Works with Factory Farms to Delay Regulation of 'Extremely Hazardous Substances,'" *In These Times*, October 6, 2004.

Roy Cordato   "'The State of the Air': Propaganda, Not Science," *Freeman: Ideas on Liberty*, October 2003.

Doug Daigle   "Dead Seas: Nutrient Pollution in Coastal Waters," *Multinational Monitor*, September 2003.

Martin Donohoe   "Factory Farms as Primary Polluter," *Z Magazine*, January 2003.

Albert L. Huebner   "The Cost of Fossil Fuels," *Humanist*, March/April 2003.

Tara Hulen   "Dispatch from Toxic Town," *OnEarth*, Winter 2003.

Randall Lutter   "Rationalizing Air Pollution Regulation," *Regulation*, Spring 2002.

Stacy Malkan   "Pollution of the People," *AlterNet*, December 26, 2004.

C. Arden Pope   "Air Pollution and Health—Good News and Bad," *New England Journal of Medicine*, September 9, 2004.

Payal Sampat   "The Hidden Threat of Groundwater Pollution," *USA Today Magazine*, July 2001.

Rob Schultheis   "The Forecast? Hazy Skies Continue," *National Parks*, January/February 2004.

Joel Schwartz   "Air Quality in U.S. Continues to Improve," *Heartland Institute*, September 1, 2003.

CHAPTER 2

Does Pollution Threaten Public Health?

Chapter Preface

One of several controversies in the debate over the impact of pollution on public health is how best to protect swimmers at America's beaches. The Environmental Protection Agency (EPA) began implementing the Beaches Environmental Assessment, Closure, and Health (BEACH) Act in 2000. The act requires that states adopt minimum water quality standards, and improve monitoring of and issue warnings about coastal water pollution. Although the act has raised water quality standards and increased reporting of unhealthy beach water, some analysts contend that these efforts are inadequate to protect America's beachgoers.

Beaches, rivers, and lakes are the number one vacation destination for Americans. Each year approximately one-fourth of the population goes swimming in these waters. Unfortunately, many Americans are unaware that such bodies of water are sometimes polluted. "People would get sick after going to the beach," claims Nancy Stoner of the National Resources Defense Council (NRDC), "but without monitoring and warning signs, they wouldn't know why." A 2002 study by the Centers for Disease Control and Prevention concluded that the incidence of infections among swimmers at America's beaches has steadily increased. According to journalists Alex Markels and Randy Dotinga, "Those who swim in tainted waters risk gastrointestinal illness that can cause nausea, vomiting, and diarrhea, as well as sinus and upper respiratory infections." Although most illnesses result from swallowing polluted water, even skin contact with tainted water can produce rashes and infect open wounds. Although most illnesses contracted after contact with polluted ocean water aren't life threatening, some beachgoers have died. "We've had a couple of cases of possible viral myocarditis," claims Jeffrey Harris, a Malibu, California, physician who has treated local surfers for this dangerous inflammation of the heart muscle. "One guy," Harris maintains, "had to have multiple heart transplants and eventually died."

Although most policymakers know that coastal pollution poses a health risk to swimmers, regulating beach water pollution is difficult because the exact source of pollution is often impossible to identify. This "nonpoint source pollution" comes from any number of sources, including aging sewage treatment and septic systems, runoff from fields and lawns saturated with fertilizers and pesticides, and storm water runoff from streets fouled by motor oil and animal waste. EPA administrators contend that little can be done if the pollution's source cannot be specifically identified. For this reason, the EPA has focused on improving the testing and reporting of polluted coastal waters.

Some commentators claim, however, that these reported results are not always accurate. "It's often a crapshoot whether the posting accurately reflects current conditions," Markels and Dotinga claim. Another problem is that the standard tests for fecal bacteria and E. coli take up to three days to yield results. According to Stanley Grant, professor of environmental engineering at the University of California, Irvine, waiting that long for results "is a lot like trying to navigate the freeways using traffic information that's two or three days old." Grant conducted a study of the water at Huntington Beach, California, and found that the warning signs were inaccurate up to 40 percent of the time.

Other analysts express concern that testing for bacteria alone may not be enough to protect swimmers. Many of the pathogens that swimmers encounter are viruses. A 2003 report by Heal the Ocean asserts, "Because the minimal infection dose of viruses is assumed to be very low, disinfected effluent free of indicator bacteria provides a false sense of safety because the effluent can still contain infectious virus at comparatively high levels." Another study conducted by the Department of Environmental Analysis and Design at the University of California, Irvine, found human adenoviruses in four out of twelve samples taken at the mouths of major rivers and creeks from Malibu to the border of Mexico in February and March 1999. The study recommends that current recreational water quality standards be improved to reflect the presence of viruses and that monitoring for human viruses be regularly conducted.

Whether stricter water testing will reduce the health risks for America's beachgoers remains to be seen. The authors in this chapter debate other controversies surrounding pollution and public health.

> *"Studies . . . point to a link between the growing number of chemicals we've been exposed to . . . and the rising incidence of health problems."*

Chemical Contaminants Threaten Public Health

Susan Freinkel

Numerous industrial pollutants permeate people's bodies today, but research on how these chemicals affect human health has been inadequate, argues Susan Freinkel in the following viewpoint. Studies show a link between rising health problems and increased exposure to chemicals, but further research is needed to determine chemicals' impact on cell development, she claims. Traditionally, Freinkel maintains, research on toxic chemicals has focused on dosage—the greater the dosage the greater the health risk—but recent studies indicate that the age at which one is exposed to the chemical determines the impact of the substance on cell development, which means that fetuses and infants may be at greater risk. Freinkel is a freelance writer from San Francisco, California.

As you read, consider the following questions:
1. In Freinkel's opinion, how many products created in chemistry labs are in active use?
2. What information is not revealed by a precise measurement of a chemical in the body, in the author's view?
3. According to the author, how do endocrine disruptors affect women?

On a bright [December 2003] morning, I drove along the coast north of San Francisco. The sky was crystal-blue, scrubbed clear by the brisk ocean winds. To the west stretched the vast expanse of the Pacific; to the east, miles of empty rolling hills. I was on my way to Bolinas, a tiny town filled with refugees from Bay Area sprawl, to visit Sharyle Patton and her husband, who moved there more than 20 years ago. Despite decades of green living, Patton, 59, recently learned her body is full of industrial pollutants.

A health activist, Patton had agreed to be tested as part of an experiment. The analysis of her blood and urine showed traces of 105 chemicals, pollutants, and pesticides, including solvents, PCBs [polychlorinated biphenyls], lead, and mercury. Most Shocking: Her levels of dioxin (a toxin emitted by incinerators) were nearly as high as those of people living in the most polluted industrial areas in America.

Like Patton, every one of us has a body loaded with chemicals. Where are they coming from? What effect are they having on our health? And, perhaps most important, what can we do about it?

Chemicals Enter Our Bodies Invisibly

Our lives are permeated by products brewed up in chemistry labs—more than 9,000 are in active use, in detergents, brake linings, and carpet pads, plastics, shampoos, and cold creams. Many of these products make our lives easier and better. But most, critics charge, have not been subjected to adequate health and safety testing. The chemicals enter our bodies through the air, the soil, our foods, and things we touch. Some pass through quickly; others, like the compounds in flame retardants, can accumulate in fatty tissue, where they persist for months or years. We even harbor vestiges of compounds that have been retired or banned. (Thirty years after the pesticide DDT was outlawed in the United States, wisps are still being detected, even in people born after the ban.) Experts call that chemical load the body burden. Even newborns have one.

[In 2003] the Centers for Disease Control and Prevention [CDC] in Atlanta [Georgia] released the most extensive body-burden study to date. Researchers tested the blood and urine samples of 2,500 people across the country and found traces of all 116 chemicals they looked for. . . . Meanwhile, the Mount Sinai School of Medicine in New York City, in collaboration with the Environmental Working Group [EWG], an advocacy organization in Washington D.C., and Commonweal, a West Coast health and environmental research institute, conducted an intensive analysis of the chemical burden in nine people, including Patton. Participants were scanned for 210 substances. The average number each harbored? Ninety-one.

A Range of Health Problems

Sounds creepy, but what does that mean? Is having traces of dioxin in my blood any more of a risk to my health than the years I smoked cigarettes or the fact that my father dropped dead of a heart attack at 63? It's awful to think that I've passed on even minute amounts of pollutants to my three children. But is their body burden a more pressing concern than making sure they steer clear of junk food, get enough exercise, and always wear seat belts? Much of the evidence is circumstantial. Several of the participants in the EWG study do have significant health problems; Patton, for instance, was never able to have children. Andrea Martin, another participant, had already survived two bouts of breast cancer when she took part in the study, and she died soon after of a brain tumor. Martin was convinced the traces of 59 carcinogens found in her body contributed to her dismal health history, but as with the other participants' illnesses, there is no direct proof.

However, . . . laboratory and epidemiological studies do point to a link between the growing number of chemicals we've been exposed to in the past 50 years and the rising incidence of health problems, including asthma, autism, various cancers, diabetes, premature births, Parkinson's disease, heart disease, infertility, and learning and attention-deficit disorders. Chemicals could even be a factor in rising obesity rates: One study found that rats exposed in utero to bisphenol A, a component of polycarbonate plastics, were significantly heavier than unexposed rats. "We certainly don't know everything about these chemicals—that's a big problem—but there's no question there are causal connections between chronic diseases and chemical exposure," says Philip Landrigan, M.D., a pediatrician and expert in environmental health at Mount Sinai.

It sounds precise to say that someone is carrying 1.79 picograms of a PCB, but the measurement tells you little. It doesn't tell you, for example, when or where or how an exposure took place. The EWG report revealed an exhaustive list of products containing the chemicals found in the volunteers' bodies—the C's alone are instructive, including: car waxes, carbon cleaners, carpet, caulking compounds, ceramics, child-proof wall finishes, chipping paint in older homes, colognes, computers, contact cements, contact lens cleaning solution, cosmetics, crystal tableware—but in most cases it's impossible to track a pollutant exactly to its source. Even when you know a product contains chemicals, finding out which ones it has is still tough. As I discovered when I began pulling out the cleaning supplies under my sink to see what I'd been unthinkingly spritzing around the house, manufacturers often don't list the chemical ingredients of their products. (The information is considered proprietary.)

What's more, body-burden tests can check for only a tiny fraction of the chemicals we're exposed to. The CDC, which has among the best testing facilities in the world, still hasn't perfected a way to detect perfluorinated compounds, one of the chemical families that most worry many experts. Abundant, persistent in the environment, and likely to accumulate in the body, these grease- and water-repelling compounds are used to make fabrics stainproof and paper cartons such as pizza boxes leakproof, and they appear, not surprisingly, to be biodegradable-proof. Most important, the results of a body-burden test can't tell you how the chemicals will interact with one another or how those combinations may affect your health. So far, few studies of such mixtures have been done.

Toxins May Affect Hormones

Though we've long known the hazards of certain chemicals, recent research suggests many may affect our health in a particularly insidious way—by disrupting our bodies' hormonal signals. To find out more about these "endocrine disrupters,"

Widespread Chemical Exposure Threatens Children

Over time, the nature of childhood illness has evolved from epidemics like scarlet fever, smallpox and measles to chronic and disabling conditions like cancer, asthma, neurological impairment and hormone disorders. Though genetic predisposition certainly plays its part, Kenneth Olden, director of the National Institute of Environmental Health Sciences, likens the gene code's influence over illness to merely loading the health risk gun. "The environment," he says, "pulls the trigger."

Environmental causes have been implicated in ailments from autism and attention deficit disorder to violent behavior, prompting widespread alarm among parents and activist groups and an unprecedented flood of research from the scientific community. "The more we learn about chemicals," says Dr. Gina Solomon, assistant clinical professor of medicine at the University of California-San Francisco, "the more we learn that very, very early in life is the most susceptible period."

Relative to their weight and size, children ingest more food, drink more water and breathe more air than adults. Their behavior only makes matters worse—children play on the ground, where there is more dust, paint chips and other dangers, and they frequently put their hands in their mouth. They also eat a much less varied diet, exposing them to concentrated pesticide residues. . . .

Children's bodies are ill-equipped to handle such a firestorm of exposure. Childhood is a period of critical organ development and fast growth. The brain growth spurt lasts all the way through age two, and once disruption occurs in the nervous system, it cannot be repaired. A child's natural defense mechanisms are not yet fully developed, especially during the first few months, and they are less able to break down certain toxins and excrete them.

Jennifer Bogo, *E Magazine*, September/October 2001.

I call John Peterson Myers, a zoologist who cowrote an influential book on the subject, titled *Our Stolen Future*. "What we need to worry about is not just cancer; it's not just mutations," he says. "It's changes in how we function, how our brain works, how well we can resist disease, how fertile we are."

Traditional toxicology focuses on the effects of high doses of toxins, when a cell's defenses are overwhelmed and the cell dies or its DNA is damaged, which can lead to cancer. But it turns out endocrine-disrupters can have devastating effects in low doses. They can "hijack control of development," says Myers, and alter the biochemical messages that determine when particular genes are turned on or off. That can have a disastrous impact during critical periods, such as when a baby's brain is developing or a preteen girl is maturing.

Toxicologists have always believed that the poison is in the dose, that if a high dose has no effect, there will be none at a low dose. But that's not true in the case of endocrine disrupters: The poison is often in the timing. Take bisphenol A, a building block of polycarbonate plastic that is used to coat the inside of aluminum cans and to make products such as Nalgene water bottles. It showed no ill effects in adult rats at high doses and seemed to be safe at 5 milligrams per day or less. Yet several newer studies have found that fetal mice exposed to doses 1,000 times lower suffer a slew of delayed reproductive effects. (When washed by hand in warm water with mild detergent, Nalgene bottles do seem to be safe for human use.)

Identifying Those at Risk

Those at greatest risk from endocrine disrupters are not adults, but preteens, infants, and fetuses. "A tiny dose of exposure during pregnancy can have much more severe effects on health than exposure during adult life," says Landrigan. The classic example is DES [diethyl-stilbestrol], an estrogen-mimicking drug and endocrine disrupter that doctors began dispensing in the 1940s to prevent miscarriages. Thirty years later, the FDA issued an advisory when the daughters of those women began turning up with vaginal cancer. (And DES sons are showing higher-than-normal rates of testicular cancer.) Many industrial chemicals, such as dioxin (found in everything from milk to fish to baby food), are equally potent estrogen mimics. . . . Animal studies have suggested prenatal exposure to dioxin can change breast tissue in such a way that tumors more easily develop decades later.

Women are hit by endocrine disrupters in particular ways. As major estrogen carriers, we're vulnerable to the many substances that mimic that hormone's actions. Women are also exposed to a raft of chemicals at work—think of the toxic substances used by manicurists, housecleaners, and even nurses—and in the personal products we use. In 2000, for instance, CDC researchers found that women between the ages of 20 and 40 had the highest levels of one member of a widely used chemical family called phthalates—a disturbing discovery because some phthalates have been found to disrupt fetal development. Why are young women's levels so high? The answer's likely to be found in the average lipstick or nail polish; phthalates are a common ingredient in cosmetics.

It's hard to talk conclusively about the effects of endocrine disrupters on people because the research has been largely on wildlife in polluted areas or on lab rats and mice, and extrapolating data across species is challenging. Critics also point out that data on the health effects are conflicting. And some toxicologists take issue with the theory that health can be affected at low doses, but not high ones. Why? Because the theory "flies in the face of generally recognized and long-standing principles of toxicology," says Richard Becker, Ph.D., a toxicologist with the American Chemistry Council. So far, he says, "the theory falls short of meeting scientific standards."

However, several major studies are under way to answer some of the most pressing questions about chemical risk. The CDC is collaborating with NASA [National Aeronautics and Space Administration] and the EPA [Environmental Protection Agency] to form a national health-tracking network to chart links between environmental hazards and disease. The National Center for Toxicogenomics is sponsoring research into the interplay between pollutants and genes. The National Institutes of Health is also gearing up the largest longitudinal study to date on the risks of chemical exposure. Researchers hope to follow 100,000 children from inception to age 21; both they and their mothers will be tested for 100-plus chemicals and their health closely monitored. . . .

Ultimately, body burden is not an individual problem, but a social one. "You can make personal lifestyle choices, and that's going to be helpful," say Sharyle Patton. "And you can avoid exposure where you can—that will be helpful. But mostly what you need to do is work at a policy level. We all have to find ways to get the world to think more carefully about how it uses chemicals."

| "*No credible scientific evidence exists to link typical exposure to chemicals in the environment with disease.*"

The Threat of Chemical Contaminants Is Exaggerated

Doug Bandow

Contrary to alarmists' claims that chemicals permeate the environment and threaten public health, exposure to dangerous chemicals has declined and human health has improved, claims Doug Bandow in the following viewpoint. Activists make spurious claims about the dangers of chemicals to frighten people into supporting strict environmental policies, Bandow contends. Exposure to chemicals does not itself pose a health risk, he maintains. In fact, he argues, no plausible evidence links disease with typical exposure to chemicals in the environment. Bandow is a senior fellow at the Cato Institute, a libertarian think tank.

As you read, consider the following questions:

1. According to Bandow, what is some of the good news about chemical exposure reported by the Centers for Disease Control?
2. In the author's view, what is the problem with animal tests?
3. What does the American Council on Science and Health report about the impact of environmental chemicals on children?

Doug Bandow, "Chemical Hysteria and Environmental Politics," *The Freeman: Ideas on Liberty*, vol. 53, July/August 2003. Copyright © 2003 by the Foundation for Economic Education, Inc. Reproduced by permission.

C hemicals are one of the wonders of human creation. They help heal and feed us; they help fuel our autos and heat our homes; they help produce toys and computers. Yet some chemicals can hurt, making them a perfect target for alarmists who detest most anything modern.

There's no doubt that chemicals have become an integral part of our lives. The Centers for Disease Control (CDC) has released its latest "National Report on Human Exposure to Environmental Chemicals," which reviewed Americans' exposure to 116 different substances. The study confirms that most people have contact with a plethora of chemicals.

Assessing Chemical Exposure and Risk

Yet this conclusion reflects the dramatic advances in bio-monitoring: scientists are now capable of detecting the minutest trace of different substances in human beings. Researchers measure concentrations of a thousandth, millionth, and billionth parts.

This enables us to better understand our environment, assess chemical exposure, and understand risks. But it also provides a tool for alarmists, who conveniently ignore actual contact levels when claiming an epidemic of chemical exposure.

At a time when many people fear for their lives, the CDC found much good news. Exposure to lead, which is particularly harmful to the development of children, and cotinine, a tobacco residue, is down.

Moreover, exposure levels to some of the most toxic chemicals were extraordinarily low. Reported the CDC: "For dioxin, furans and coplanar PCBs [polychlorinated biphenyls], most people in the Second Report had levels that were below what the analytic method could detect."

Even the bad news was bad mainly relative to overall successes. For instance, during the 1990s cotinine exposure dropped 55 percent for teens, 58 percent for kids, and 75 percent for adults; yet today the exposure of black children remains disproportionately high.

A Pattern of Fear Mongering

Alas, good news does not dampen the alarmist impulse in some people. The Environmental Working Group (EWG) conducted its own study and found an average of "91 indus-trial compounds, pollutants, and other chemicals" in the nine volunteers studied. All told, the EWG reported 167 different chemicals, many of which, it claimed, caused can-cer, birth defects, or other harms. The result was a signifi-cant "body burden," as the group put it.

But this is fear-mongering at its misleading worst. Simple exposure demonstrates nothing. As the CDC explained: "Just because people have an environmental chemical in their blood or urine does not mean that the chemical causes disease."

This is the case even for substances known to be capable of causing harm. Observes Elizabeth Whelan, president of the American Council on Science and Health (ACSH), people "should remember the basic tenet of toxicology—the dose makes the poison." Almost anything can prove toxic if ingested in a high-enough concentration, one vastly above the levels faced by even the most at-risk person.

Yet animal tests not only rely on huge dosage levels, but also can fall afoul of the substantial differences between ro-dents and primates. In many cases absorption rates and hor-monal reactions, which vary among creatures, matter far more than exposure levels.

Todd Seavey of ACSH argues, "Thanks to the CDC re-port, we're now more certain than ever that the synthetic chemical amounts we are routinely subjected to are trivial. We ought to feel safer than ever."

The Problem with Junk Science

Another argument has been advanced by groups like the Col-laborative on Health and the Environment (CHE), an um-brella group for the most active alarmists. It claims that multi-ple chemical exposure can be harmful—indeed, that chemicals are currently hurting one-third of the population. CHE is aided by the PR firm Fenton Communications, which special-izes in turning junk science into newspaper headlines.

It's an attractive argument for the scientifically unin-formed, but it fails the basic test of evidence. As Steven Mil-loy, publisher of JunkScience.com, points out: "Despite more than 40 years and countless billions of dollars of re-search, no credible scientific evidence exists to link typical exposures to chemicals in the environment with disease."

Indeed, though our theoretical exposure to chemicals has increased dramatically over the last half century, actual chemical contamination of the environment has been falling. And we are living longer and healthier lives than ever. Apparently the human body is able to bear the alleged chemical burden.

Are Children at Risk?

What of children? People naturally worry about the impact on youthful development, but ACSH warns, "We are at a juncture where emotion, fear, and uncertainty compete with scientific data, toxicological principles, and principles of risk analysis." In fact, ACSH reports in a new book, *Are Children More Vulnerable to Environmental Chemicals?*, "There is little toxicological evidence to support the premise that children are consistently more susceptible to environmental chemicals than adults."

A Cause Without a Disease

As public fear mounted, the evidence for a creeping epidemic caused by endocrine disruptors in the environment remained elusive. Although most scientists now acknowledge that many substances can have an effect on the human endocrine system, more recent analysis has shown that many of the claims about health effects were either exaggerated or based on flawed analysis of observations. As Stephen H. Safe, Professor of Veterinary Physiology and Pharmacology and of Biochemistry and Biophysics at Texas A&M University (College Station, TX, USA) put it: "The hypothesis is okay, but we don't even have a problem."

Holger Breithaupt, *EMBO Reports*, 2004.

Where there is a problem, as with lead and PCBs, kids need to be protected. But parents need not live in fear of a world that is actually getting safer and healthier day by day. And they need to be aware of what ACSH warns as a "disturbing pattern in which activists with a nonscience agenda manipulate the public's legitimate and appropriate concern for children's health in an effort to promote legislation, litigation, and regulation."

This is the fundamental problem. Alarmist groups with radical political agendas are ever-ready to manipulate science to promote their own ends. A particularly apt example is the case of acrylamide, a chemical coagulant used in drinking water, wastewater treatment, and tunnel construction. In April 2002 the Swedish National Food Administration and researchers at Stockholm University held a press conference announcing that disturbingly high levels of acrylamide had been found in food. The revelation set off a media sensation around the world. French fries and potato chips cause cancer! California environmental activists sued snack-food makers and fast-food restaurants to warn customers that their products included a chemical "known to the State of California to cause cancer."

Acrylamide is formed naturally in the cooking of many foods. It appears to cause cancer in rodents fed exceptionally high doses. In fact, in this case the doses not only well-exceeded human consumption, but they also may have exceeded medically tolerable levels for mice, since more died from other causes than from cancer.

Moreover, extrapolating such results to humans is always problematic: genetic differences between rodents and primates often result in different metabolic reactions to chemicals. Dr. Joseph Rosen of Rutgers University observes: "There is substantial evidence that the rodent studies may not be accurately predicting relevance to human health."

The [January 2003] *British Journal of Cancer* published a study announcing that there was no apparent link between acrylamide in food and cancer. One British newspaper headline trumpeted: "Crisps Do Not Cause Cancer!" A Swedish paper went onto suggest that acrylamide in food might actually reduce cancer risks.

Obviously, some substances do cause cancer, and evidence of carcinogenic properties requires investigation. But as Waldemar Ingdahl puts it, "Publication by press conference is not good scientific publishing," especially when there is a transparent political agenda. Constantly crying wolf will make it harder to deal with the few cases where there is a legitimate health issue.

"The evidence pointing to air pollution as one major culprit [in the asthma epidemic] is getting harder and harder to ignore."

Air Pollution May Contribute to the Increased Incidence of Asthma

Kimi Eisele

Studies have linked the increased incidence of asthma in the United States with air pollution, maintains Kimi Eisele in the following viewpoint. Researchers have long known that air pollution triggers asthma attacks, she claims, but some studies reveal a direct connection. In one study, Eisele asserts, children raised in highly polluted communities developed more cases of asthma than those living in communities with clean air. Air pollution policies should acknowledge this connection, Eisele argues. Eisele, a poet and nonfiction writer, is managing editor of *110°*, a magazine produced by Tucson, Arizona, teenagers.

As you read, consider the following questions:

1. In Eisele's view, in what ways do asthmatics have to pay particular attention to their surroundings?
2. According to the author, what percentage of the patients who visit the Phoenix Children's Hospital Breathmobile are Hispanic?
3. How has the meaning of asthma changed for the author as an adult?

When I was eight years old, I bit into a red apple and my throat closed. It was an autumn morning, and I was sitting in the back seat of the car. My mouth began to itch and I felt like I had to burp, but I couldn't. I could barely speak. Outside, dry leaves were scuttling across the sidewalk. I couldn't get enough air. My parents, twisting around in alarm to look at me from the front seat, started inhaling and exhaling deeply and slowly, as if modeling breathing would remind me how to do it. But I hadn't forgotten how to breathe. I simply couldn't.

Soon afterward, I was diagnosed with atopic asthma—asthma caused by allergies, which is a chronic condition with no known cure. The word asthma comes from the Greek word for "panting," which is what we asthmatics do when we're trying to get air. My own panting is induced by any number of factors: dust mite dung, dry wind, cat dander, cold air, rabbits, wood smoke, pollen, guinea pigs, cigarettes, grass, horses, and some species of trees, among other things. Any of these will make my eyes itch, my nose run, and my skin break out in a rash. Or they will shut my airways.

Because I have asthma, for most of my life I've had to pay attention to my surroundings. I've had to be aware of hovering dust, the direction of a spring breeze, the presence of a cat. Luckily, my asthma is mild. My attacks aren't life-threatening, and as long as I have my inhaler along, they're easily relieved. And I can usually get myself out of the path of the allergens, away from the cats and rabbits, in from the pollens, and into a "clean" air space.

More than Just a Trigger?

But for the 17 million other people with asthma in the United States, controlling the air space is not always so simple, especially because some of the most common triggers of asthma—smog and soot from tailpipe exhaust and power plants—are in the air we breathe every day.

It's possible that air pollution is doing more than just triggering asthma attacks. It may also be an element in the development of the disease—a criminal accomplice, not just an accessory after the fact. In industrialized countries, asthma is becoming more common and more severe. Five thousand people die of it every year in the United States. Currently it's the sixth most common chronic condition in the nation. Three times as many people have it now as in 1980. Some 6 million of them are children. For children, asthma is the most common chronic disorder, the leading cause of missed school, and the leading cause of hospitalization.

Is polluted air helping to drive this epidemic? As yet, there's no scientific consensus. But the evidence pointing to air pollution as one major culprit is getting harder and harder to ignore. . . .

Studying the Causes

Several long-term, multimillion-dollar studies are now underway to track children from the womb onward, measuring precisely what contaminants they're exposed to and recording who develops asthma and who doesn't. One study will investigate effects of the mix of air pollutants and pesticides that descends on children in central California . . . This research should start to shape concrete answers. . . .

[In February 2002] researchers from the University of Southern California published the most persuasive evidence yet linking asthma and air pollution. The study followed more than 3,500 children from twelve Southern California communities, six of which endured the kind of smog for which the Los Angeles region is notorious, and six of which had fairly clean air. Smog's primary ingredient is ozone, a caustic gas formed when sunlight and heat acts on certain air pollutants—namely, nitrogen oxides and hydrocarbons. In Southern California, by far the largest source of these pollutants is tailpipes.

Drawing Conclusions

None of the children had asthma when the study began. After five years, 265 were diagnosed with it. But the critical finding was that children who lived in high-ozone areas and were involved in several team sports were three times more likely to develop asthma than couch potatoes living in less polluted communities. "Kids playing three or more sports are likely to be outdoors ventilating at high rates, and are therefore being exposed to higher levels of air pollution," explains James Gauderman, one of the study's authors.

But it's only a beginning. Martinez is one researcher who says the findings are important but not conclusive. High rates of asthma in cities may be related to factors such as stress, he argues. And he points out that asthma comes in different varieties. In the days when East Germany was highly polluted, its population had higher rates of asthma—but fewer allergies—than West Germans. It's possible, Martinez says, that pollution is not a risk factor for the allergic form of the disease, but may be a factor for another form of the disease.

A Polluted City

Phoenix, Arizona, a fast-growing, sprawling desert city, is one of the most ozone-polluted cities in the country. In mid-September [2002], not long after dawn, I drive there to visit the Breathmobile, a mobile asthma clinic of the Phoenix Children's Hospital. Though the desert air feels crisp at this hour, from the highway I can see the thick green-gray stripe of smog that has already spread across the horizon. On especially polluted days, flashing signs on the road are turned on to warn drivers that the air is bad.

Children in Phoenix's urban schools have a lot of asthma. Maricopa County, where the city is located, has one of the highest death rates of asthma in the nation—2.1 percent in 1999.

This morning the Breathmobile is at William T. Machan Elementary School. To get there, I drive through a residential neighborhood with tree-lined streets, single-story homes, and semi-green lawns. Though it doesn't fit the stereotype, this is an inner-city school. Downtown Phoenix and its heavy automobile traffic are only blocks away. Students here face the same challenges that children in most inner cities in America face: low family incomes, poor access to health care, and abnormally high rates of asthma. . . .

Children in Danger

Fifth-grader Elizabeth Vargas, back for a checkup, is the first patient of the day. Her lungs don't look good. Each time she exhales into a tube connected to the computer, its screen shows a picture of a balloon being blown up. A healthy child would be able to pop the balloon. But until Elizabeth inhales the bronchiodilator medication albuterol, she can pop only two out of five balloons. After her appointment, Elizabeth will take home a supply of Advair, a steroid-based preventive daily medication. Unless her asthma becomes less severe as she grows up, as sometimes happens, she may have to take it for the rest of her life.

The Dangers of Diesel

Diesel emissions affect all people, but children are particularly vulnerable. Outdoors more often than adults, children's small bodies and maturing lungs experience greater exposure to harmful air pollutants. New studies in California find that air pollution not only exacerbates children's asthma, but may actually cause asthma in otherwise healthy children. And Yale researchers found that the air inside diesel school buses contained 5 to 15 times more toxic soot than the outside air.

Union of Concerned Scientists, "Pollution from School Buses May Be Hazardous to Your Health: The Diesel Dilemma," www.ucsusa.org, 2004.

Elizabeth is a typical Breathmobile patient. Like her, 75 percent of the Breathmobile's patients are Hispanic. Also like her, many of them get their first real medical help here. Elizabeth has suffered from tight lungs all her life, so much so that when [Breathmobile director Judy] Harris asks in Spanish what happens when she runs, she answers, "My lungs get agitated, and it hurts here"—putting a hand to the center of her chest. She missed thirty days of school last winter because of asthma. Yet her condition went undiagnosed until her first visit to the clinic several months ago.

When asthma gripped my own lungs, I had the middle-class advantages of good air—we lived on a quiet street in a small college town—and good health care. My parents even bought a special vacuum cleaner that sucked dust into a vat of water so it wouldn't blow back into the house. But today, those who lack such socioeconomic cushions suffer disproportionately from asthma. This fact infuriates many environmental justice advocates, who believe the link between asthma and air pollution is as obvious as the sooty air in inner-city neighborhoods.

"It's certainly no accident that the neighborhoods with the

highest rates of asthma also have a high incidence of polluting facilities, and that they're also low-income communities of color," says Omar Freilla. Freilla works at Sustainable South Bronx, a New York City group that seeks to reduce pollution and promote parks in one of the city's most environmentally blighted areas. The South Bronx, he points out, is the site of twenty-six waste facilities and the largest food distribution center in the world. The number of trucks passing through the food distribution center's neighborhood has been estimated at 11,000 daily. And Freilla believes that the asthma hospitalization rate in the South Bronx—six times higher than the national average—is directly related to all those tailpipes. . . .

The Politics of Pollution

To breathe is to live. But for us asthmatics, when the air is full of pollens and particulates, what we need most becomes our worst enemy. When I was young, asthma meant only my personal affliction and the chores it demanded: regulating my breath, paying attention to allergens, and medicating. But as an adult, I'm implicated. If air pollution causes asthma, what does that mean about the energy I use and the car I drive? What does it mean that 6 million children in the United States have trouble breathing? I know I'm supposed to stay calm. But the evidence and the reality of it make me want to hyperventilate.

Michael Lerner, of the health and environmental research organization Commonweal, says the new air pollution research has "enormous political salience." He adds, "Parents are agonizingly aware of the reality that their children can't breathe, and of the tremendous impact that has on a child's life—on their ability to participate in sports and live childhood the way childhood is meant to be lived."

And then there's this: While the scientists continue their studies, the rest of us are left to control our breath. Air pollution is a hazard for many asthmatics, whether it caused our asthma or not. "We have enough data now on air pollution and asthma and mortality to say we need to be moving in the direction of more control [of pollution]," says Jonathan Samet of Johns Hopkins University. "Would another finding make a difference?"

"*[The Environmental Protection Agency's]
asthma-pollution connection is
exaggerated.*"

The Link Between Air Pollution and Asthma Is Exaggerated

Ben Lieberman

In order to promote stricter air pollution policies, government entities such as the Environmental Protection Agency exaggerate the connection between the increased incidence of asthma and air pollution, argues Ben Lieberman in the following viewpoint. Ozone concentrations and particulate matter, which make air pollution dangerous, have declined, Lieberman maintains, which suggests another explanation for the rise in asthma rates. In fact, he claims, new research reveals that indoor air pollution may explain the increase. Lieberman is a senior policy analyst at the Competitive Enterprise Institute, a libertarian think tank.

As you read, consider the following questions:

1. According to Lieberman, what vehicle emissions did the Clinton administration hope to target by exaggerating the connection between asthma and air pollution?
2. What types of indoor air pollutants may be the primary culprit in the development or worsening of asthma symptoms in susceptible people, in the author's view?
3. In the author's opinion, what is disturbing about exploiting childhood asthma for bureaucratic gain?

Ben Lieberman, "Exploiting Asthmatic Children," *The Freeman: Ideas on Liberty*, vol. 50, August 2000. Copyright © 2000 by the Foundation for Economic Education, Inc. Reproduced by permission.

C hildhood asthma is on the rise, and the experts are not sure why. The Environmental Protection Agency [EPA] blames air pollution, and uses concerns about asthmatic children to justify its aggressive implementation of the Clean Air Act. In contrast, a recent National Academy of Sciences report points to indoor, not outdoor, contaminants as the likely cause. If the National Academy is right, EPA is wasting billions on misdirected solutions to this very real problem.

In 1997, EPA ran into some trouble promoting its tough new ambient air-quality standards for ozone and particulate matter (smog and soot). Even the agency's own Clean Air Scientific Advisory Committee concluded that tightening the already strict existing standards will garner few if any additional public health benefits. With such a weak factual case for action, [then] EPA Administrator Carol Browner switched to emotional arguments, claiming that the new rules would prevent "hundreds of thousands of cases of significantly decreased lung function in children and cases of aggravated asthma."

Gaining Support for New Rules

EPA's asthma-pollution connection is exaggerated. In fact, over the same 25-year span that childhood asthma incidence and mortality has approximately doubled, ambient concentrations of ozone and particulate matter have substantially declined. Sidestepping the evidence, the agency misused the issue to gain support for its costly new rules, and it worked—at least until a federal court invalidated them [in 1999]. The case is headed to the Supreme Court.

[In 1999,] those same asthmatic children were said to be suffering because of sport utility vehicles. In December [1999], EPA enacted new motor vehicle emissions standards, including far stricter ones for SUVs. During a press conference announcing the rules, [then] President [Bill] Clinton told a group of Washington, D.C., elementary-school students that "Carol Browner has said to me, you have got to do something to reduce incidents of asthma and other respiratory diseases among young children." According to [then] Vice President [Al] Gore, EPA's tightened emissions standards will result in "260,000 fewer asthma attacks in children, and more than 4,000 fewer premature deaths."

[In November 1999,] EPA and the Department of Justice announced the filing of lawsuits against 17 midwestern and southern electric power plants, claiming, among other things, that their emissions carve a childhood asthma path that stretches all the way to the northeast. [Then] Attorney General Janet Reno stated that "when children can't breathe because of pollution from a utility plant hundreds of miles away, something must be done." As of May 2000, over 40 such coal-fired facilities have been targeted with lawsuits or administrative actions.

Evidence That Exposure to Some Indoor Substances Can Trigger or Worsen Asthma

A . . . report from the Institute of Medicine (IOM) of the National Academies finds strong, causal evidence linking common indoor substances to the triggering or worsening of asthma symptoms in susceptible people. It also finds that a variety of strategies, such as removing a pet, intensive cleaning, prohibiting smoking, and controlling indoor humidity, often helps to alleviate asthma symptoms.

After reviewing the latest scientific studies, the committee that wrote the report concluded that exposure to allergens produced by house dust mites—found in nearly every indoor environment—can lead to asthma in children who are predisposed to developing the disease. In addition, exposure to these allergens, as well as those produced by cats and cockroaches, can aggravate symptoms in some asthma sufferers. The condition of asthmatic preschoolers also can be worsened by contact with secondhand tobacco smoke.

"The prevalence of asthma continues to rise dramatically in this country", said committee chair Richard B. Johnston Jr., professor, department of pediatrics, University of Colorado School of Medicine, and National Jewish Medical and Research Center, Denver. "People spend most of their time inside, and it's vital that we understand how the indoor environment may contribute to the disease. Fortunately there are actions people can take to limit their exposure and ease symptoms".

Health and Energy Company, http://healthandenergy.com, 2000.

It appears that EPA and its allies will play the childhood asthma card again and again, as long as it wins. The issue . . . even [became] a part of the [2000] presidential race, with

Sierra Club television ads blaming the suffering of young asthmatics in Texas on [then] Governor [George W.] Bush's supposedly weak enforcement of air-quality standards.

The Primary Culprit

Obviously, not all of these putative causes of childhood asthma can be as significant as claimed, and it is quite possible that none of them are. Building on a growing body of evidence, "Clearing the Air: Asthma and Indoor Air Exposures," by the National Academy's Institute of Medicine, makes a compelling case that indoor air pollutants, such as insect remains and molds, are the primary culprit. Though the report does not directly compare the relative contributions of indoor and outdoor air, it found "strong, causal evidence linking common indoor substances to the development or worsening of asthma symptoms in susceptible people."

As for why asthma has been on the increase, several other studies have blamed the federal government's policy of promoting tighter, more energy-efficient residences, schools, and other buildings in response to the energy crisis of the 1970s. These efforts may have had the unintended consequence of trapping more pollutants indoors, including several now implicated as asthma triggers. Unfortunately, the Clinton administration [was at the time] stepping up its energy efficiency agenda in the name of fighting global warming, seemingly oblivious to the downside of heavily insulated and less well-ventilated homes.

Indoor Air Experts

Even EPA's own indoor air experts concede that "indoor levels of many pollutants may be two to five times, and on occasion more than one hundred times, higher than outdoor levels," and that "most people spend as much as 90 percent of their time indoors." Indeed, EPA funded the Institute of Medicine study as well as others implicating indoor air pollution as a health threat. Clearly, the agency is knowingly overstating the public health benefits of many rules targeting outdoor pollutants.

Public concerns about the increase in childhood asthma are entirely justified. Indeed, it is hard to think of anything more important than the health of children. That's why it is so disturbing to see the issue being exploited for bureaucratic gain.

Every dollar spent fighting an overblown asthma threat is a dollar that can't be used to make real progress. Keep that in mind the next time the EPA announces a new measure to "protect" the asthmatic children.

"A spectrum of human health effects has been observed following mercury exposure."

Mercury Contamination Poses a Serious Health Threat

Physicians for Social Responsibility

In the following viewpoint Physicians for Social Responsibility, a public policy organization comprised of medical and public health professionals, contends that pervasive mercury contamination threatens the health of millions of Americans. Mercury released into the environment by smokestacks ultimately makes its way into bodies of water and accumulates in fish, the authors assert. Mothers who consume contaminated fish pass mercury on to their unborn children, where it targets their developing nervous systems, resulting in low birth weight, mental retardation, and other birth defects, the authors maintain. Young children whose brains are still developing are also susceptible to the toxic effects of mercury.

As you read, consider the following questions:

1. How does methylmercury interfere with the developing fetal nervous system, in the opinion of Physicians for Social Responsibility?
2. According to the authors, why might children have higher exposures to mercury than might adults?
3. In the authors' view, what are some of the effects of adult exposure to methylmercury?

Mercury is a naturally occurring metal. It can take a variety of forms, including the familiar silvery metal elemental form, inorganic salts that have been used in medications and industrial compounds, and organic forms. A spectrum of human health effects has been observed following mercury exposure, with the severity depending on the type of mercury, the amount, and the timing of exposure. Though some people may come in contact with elemental or inorganic mercury in their homes or workplaces, by far the most common type of mercury exposure is dietary exposure to methylmercury, an organic form that is a common contaminant of fish and shellfish.

Methylmercury is formed when elemental mercury—such as that emitted from industrial smokestacks or spilled from broken thermometers—makes its way into rivers, lakes, and oceans. There, aquatic microbes convert it to methylmercury through a biochemical reaction. Methylmercury then accumulates in many edible freshwater and ocean fish species. It is estimated that human activities such as mining, trash incineration, and burning coal to produce electricity have tripled the amount of mercury released into the environment annually.

Methylmercury Exposure and Human Health

Methylmercury was first made in the laboratory in the mid 19th century, but when two laboratory workers died of methylmercury poisoning, the compound was abandoned for decades. It made a comeback in the 20th century as a potent antifungal agent, but again was abandoned after several serious poisoning episodes affected thousands of people from the 1950s to the 1970s. While several organ systems in the body can be affected by methylmercury, the major target system is the central nervous system, and the most vulnerable life stage is fetal. Data are accumulating that suggest that the cardiovascular system may also be an important target for methylmercury toxicity at low levels of exposure. Adverse effects differ depending upon the age at exposure.

Methylmercury is a potent neurotoxicant that interferes with brain development. It readily crosses the placenta, and fetal blood levels are equal to or slightly higher than maternal levels. It is actively transported into the brain, where it interferes with nerve cell differentiation and division by binding to DNA and RNA. It also interferes with nerve cell migration and prevents the development of normal brain structure. High-dose exposures during fetal development can result in low birth weight, small head circumference, severe mental retardation, cerebral palsy, deafness, blindness, and seizures. Severely affected children may be born to mothers who exhibited no symptoms of methylmercury exposure during pregnancy.

Lower-dose prenatal exposure from maternal consumption of fish and marine mammals may cause more subtle neurodevelopmental damage that is not expressed until later in childhood. . . . Epidemiologic studies of infant-mother pairs in the Faroe Islands have found deficits on neurobehavioral tests, particularly on tests of attention, fine motor function, language, visual-spatial abilities (e.g., drawing), and memory that correlate with prenatal mercury exposure. A similar investigation of infant-mother pairs in Seychelles failed to find a correlation. The National Research Council did an exhaustive evaluation of the studies and concluded that the conflicting results might be due to differences in methodology, types of exposures, and populations studies, but that the proper public health approach was to use the positive Faroe Island studies as the basis for setting safe exposure levels.

In addition to exposure *in utero*, infants and children ingest methylmercury from breast milk and other foods in their diet. Young children and infants are potentially more susceptible to neurotoxicity from methylmercury than older children and adults because the brain continues to grow and develop dramatically for the first several years of life. Children also may have higher exposures than adults pound for pound, because a child eats more food relative to his or her body weight than an adult does. As a result, they may have higher exposure and thus higher risk than adults do.

Adult Neurological Effects

The mature nervous system can be adversely and permanently affected by methylmercury. Autopsy results have shown that methylmercury causes nerve cell death and scarring in selected areas of the brain. Symptoms are nonspecific, often delayed for months following exposure, and the severity of effects increases with increased exposure. Effects with low to moderate chronic exposure range from paresthesias (abnormal sensations such as numbness and tingling of fingers, toes, mouth, and lips) to ataxia (stumbling or clumsy gait) and generalized weakness, to decreased vision and hearing, spasticity, tremor, and finally coma and death with higher, more acute exposures. Diagnosis depends on the clinician having a high index of suspicion, identifying the source of exposure, and evaluating blood and hair mercury levels. . . . Clinic-based studies have raised concern that high-end fish consumers in the United States may be ingesting enough methylmercury to cause clinical illness.

Cardiovascular Effects

Data are evolving in support of a link between methylmercury exposure and increased risk of high blood pressure, heart-rate abnormalities, and heart disease. These effects are seen following exposure during fetal development, as well as in adulthood. While studies conflict, it is of particular concern since the effects may occur at levels similar to those known to cause neurological damage. More research is required to define these effects fully.

How Widespread Are the Effects?

Mercury contamination in fish across the United States is so pervasive that health departments in 45 states have issued fish consumption advisories. In addition, 11 states have consumption advisories for every inland water body for at least one fish species, and eight states have statewide coastal marine advisories for king mackerel. [As of 2004,] 11 states have also issued advisories urging women and children to limit consumption of canned tuna.

A . . . study released by the Centers for Disease Control and Prevention details the levels of mercury and 115 other environmental contaminants measured in the blood and urine from a representative sample of American adults and children. According to the second National Report on Human Exposure to Environmental Chemicals, almost 8% of women of childbearing ages (16 to 49) have levels of mercury that exceed what is considered safe for a fetus. Across the entire U.S. population, this could mean that millions of children are at risk.

| *"Higher blood mercury concentrations were . . . not associated with specific patterns of health complaints."'*

There Is No Evidence Linking Mercury Contamination with Health Problems

Steven Milloy

There is no scientific evidence proving that consuming fish containing typical concentrations of mercury threatens human health, claims Steven Milloy in the following viewpoint. Food and Drug Administration guidelines that suggest people limit their consumption of fish to protect themselves and their children from mercury contamination are not based on science, he argues. In fact, Milloy contends, these rules may prevent people from consuming fish, which is part of a healthy diet. Milloy is an adjunct scholar with the Cato Institute, a libertarian think tank, and author of *Junk Science Judo: Self-Defense Against Health Scares and Scams.*

As you read, consider the following questions:
1. According to Milloy, what fish did the Food and Drug Administration recommend Americans not eat?
2. To what were Japanese women in Minamata Bay exposed during the 1950s, in the author's view?
3. In the author's opinion, what does the FDA apparently want Americans to think about local bodies of water?

The Food and Drug Administration [FDA] . . . issued a . . . warning to pregnant women about mercury in seafood. You can "protect your baby" from developmental harm by following three rules, claims the FDA.

But there's no evidence the rules will protect anyone and they're only likely to foster undue concern about an important part of our food supply.

"Do not eat shark, swordfish, king mackerel or tilefish because they contain high levels of mercury," is the FDA's first rule.

It's certainly true such larger fish tend to have higher levels of mercury in their tissue since mercury levels tend to accumulate up the food chain. But unless women are consuming fish that have been exposed to industrial-level concentrations of mercury for extended periods—as Japanese women in the vicinity of Minamata Bay did during the 1950s—it's not at all clear consuming large fish is any health risk.

Examining the Evidence

Researchers from the Harvard School of Public Health recently reported in the *Journal of Occupational and Environmental Medicine* (February 2002) that they could not find mercury-related health effects among a group of regular swordfish consumers.

Although a "significant relationship between fish consumption and blood mercury concentrations" was identified by the researchers, "higher blood mercury concentrations were, however, not associated with specific patterns of health complaints."

There also is no evidence of a general threat to infants and children from typical maternal consumption of fish with typical mercury concentrations.

"No evidence of adverse effect from either pre- or postnatal exposure to methyl mercury," is how Thomas W. Carson of the University of Rochester School of Medicine characterizes the results of an ongoing study of children in the Seychelles Islands.

In fact, "a surprising finding in the results of the examination of children at 66 months of age was that several [intelligence] tests scores improved as either pre- or postnatal mercury levels increased . . . linear regression analysis reveals statistically significant beneficial correlations," noted Dr. Carson.

That's exactly the opposite situation of what the FDA claims as the basis of its warning.

"A Whole Lot Abalone"

Although U.S. mercury emissions have fallen 42% over the past decade, a Princeton University study found no change in mercury levels in Pacific tuna since 1970. Even if the world got rid of every power plant, fish still would ingest mercury, because 55% of the world's emissions of the element come from nature. Studies of 550-year-old Aleutian mummies show they contained more mercury than do people today. As one pundit put it, "It's a whole lot abalone."

Robert Peltier, *Power*, October 2004.

Aside from Minamata Bay, not a single clinical case of mercury poisoning associated with fish consumption is to be found in the scientific literature, according to Dr. Carson.

It seems FDA is warning (scaring?) us about a scenario that has, essentially, never occurred.

Arbitrary Rules

The FDA's other two rules are similarly not grounded in science.

"Levels of mercury in other fish can vary. You can safely eat up to 12 ounces (2 to 3 meals) of other purchased fish and shellfish per week. Mix up the types of fish and shellfish you eat and do not eat the same type of fish and shellfish more than once a week," warns the FDA's second rule.

Now where did the 12 ounces-per-week figure come from? Is there evidence that consuming 13 ounces per week—or for that matter, 130 ounces per week—is dangerous? Is there evidence eating the same type of fish and shellfish more than once a week is harmful?

The FDA's 12 ounces-per-week rule is simply arbitrary.

The third FDA rule reads, "Check local advisories about the safety of fish caught by family and friends in your local rivers and streams. If no advice is available, you can safely eat up to 6 ounces (one meal) per week of fish you catch from local waters, but don't consume any other fish during that week."

The FDA apparently wants us to think any given local body of water is a potential Minamata Bay, where tons of mercury were dumped into the water over two decades. But even if such situations existed in the U.S.—and they never have—the Minamata Bay mercury poisoning victims no doubt consumed much more than 6 ounces of fish weekly.

Seafood is definitely part of a healthy diet. Further, the seafood industry is a large part of our economy. Unless the FDA has a science-based health warning to issue, it should clam up.

Periodical Bibliography

The following articles have been selected to supplement the diverse views presented in this chapter.

Robert G. Arnold	"Pharmaceuticals Without a Prescription," *Journal of Environmental Engineering*, October 2002.
Jennifer Bogo	"Children at Risk: Widespread Chemical Exposure Threatens Our Most Vulnerable Population," *E Magazine*, September/October 2001.
Zach Corrigan	"Mercury and Bush's Not-So-Clear Skies," *Multinational Monitor*, April 2003.
Robert E. Criss and M. Lee Davisson	"Fertilizers, Water Quality, and Human Health," *Environmental Health Perspectives*, July 2004.
Mark H. Hyman	"The Impact of Mercury on Human Health and the Environment," *Alternative Therapies*, November/December 2004.
Melissa Knopper	"Drugging Our Water," *E Magazine*, January/February 2003.
David Lean	"Mercury Pollution a Mind-Numbing Problem," *Canadian Chemical News*, January 2003.
Alex Markels and Randy Dotinga	"Don't Go in the Water," *U.S. News & World Report*, August 16, 2004.
R.L. Maynard	"Asthma and Urban Air Pollution," *Clinical and Experimental Allergy*, 2001.
John Peterson Myers	"From Silent Spring to Scientific Revolution," *Yes!* Spring 2003.
Robert Peltier	"Mercury Mockery," *Power*, October 2004.
Whitney Royster	"Dumping Diesel: Cleaner Fuels Will Save Thousands from Illness and Help All of Us Breathe Easier," *OnEarth*, Summer 2004.
Joel Schwartz	"Air Pollution and Children's Health," *Pediatrics*, April 2004.
James M. Taylor	"Health Threat of Mercury Overblown, Scientists Say," *Heartland Institute*, May 1, 2004.
Lori Valigra	"How Safe Is the Water?" *Christian Science Monitor*, December 30, 2004.

CHAPTER 3

How Can Society Reduce Pollution?

Chapter Preface

One way that society can reduce pollution is to insist that electronics producers ensure that electronic waste is responsibly recycled. According to journalist Matthew Power, "Due to our hunger for increased processing speeds and ever more stunning graphics, the working life of a computer is now roughly two years; it is estimated that by 2006, some 163,240 computers, weighing 3,513 tons, will become obsolete in America every day." Many consumers turn in obsolete computers for recycling, and most believe that they are acting responsibly by doing so. However, many recycled computers end up in developing nations, where extremely hazardous e-waste recycling operations pollute the air, water, and soil. In "Exporting Harm: The High-Tech Trashing of Asia," a coalition of environmental activists contends, "Fifty to 80 percent of electronics waste collected for recycling in the U.S. is sent to China, India, Pakistan or other developing countries where it is processed for recycling in largely unregulated and environmentally horrific conditions."

Toxic e-waste recycling operations in developing nations threaten the environment and people's health. Computers turned in by consumers for recycling contain 6.3 billion pounds of plastics, 1.6 billion pounds of lead, 630,000 pounds of mercury, and a host of other hazardous elements, including cadmium, barium, and arsenic. Gleaners, whose job it is to harvest valuable elements in obsolete computers, are exposed to these toxic chemicals, as are the people in the surrounding community. For example, after removing the copper yoke on a cathode-ray-tube (CRT) monitor, gleaners in Guiyu, China, a village near Hong Kong, smash and dump the remainder of the leaded glass into local waters. "Independent tests by investigators from BAC [Basel Action Network] and Greenpeace found levels of lead in Guiyu's river that were 190 times the safe limit for drinking water," Power maintains. To harvest the gold in a circuit board, gleaners, wearing no protective clothing or ventilators, immerse the board in molten lead-tin solder that has been heated in a wok over an open coal fire. The gleaner then removes the silicon chips with pliers. To get to the trace amounts of gold, they drench the chips with hydrochloric and nitric acid. The acidic sludge is then dumped into the surrounding soil. "One test site in Guiyi found a soil pH of 0," Power claims. When soil pH is low, it becomes a poor medium for growing plants. To collect the copper in sheathed wires, the wires are burned in open ditches, releasing carcinogenic dioxins and furans into the air. As a result, "Chinese media have reported elevated levels of tuberculosis, birth defects, and respiratory problems [in Guiyu]," Power reports.

Some commentators contend that electronics manufacturers should be held responsible for the toxic e-waste they produce. EcoCycle, a Colorado recycling company, argues that the United States should adopt a program similar to Extended Producer Responsibility (EPR), a European e-waste program. EPR makes the producer legally and financially responsible for the end-of-life management of their products. "If this were to become one of the rules by which [American] business must play, they would be making many more products and packaging that are recyclable, compostable or reusable," EcoCycle argues. Moreover, those who advocate producer responsibility contend that manufacturers of electronic products should help pay the cost of recycling their products in an environmentally responsible way. In "Exporting Harm," the authors maintain, "As long as manufacturers can evade the ultimate costs of their hazardous products via export to Asia, they can delay aggressively deploying their ingenuity to make sure their products are less toxic and burdensome to the planet."

Deciding exactly who should be responsible for e-waste illustrates how difficult it can be to determine who should bear the cost of reducing pollution. The authors in the following chapter debate several methods proposed to reduce pollution.

> "Compared to landfilling, recycling is the
> economic and environmental favorite by a
> long shot."

Recycling Is an Effective Way
to Deal with Waste

Sam Martin

Recycling is better for the environment than dumping
America's trash into landfills, argues Sam Martin in the following viewpoint. The liners that prevent toxic landfill
chemicals from leaking into America's water supply eventually break down, Martin maintains. Recycling also makes
more environmental sense than producing products from
virgin materials, he contends. Cutting down trees for paper
and manufacturing plastics from petroleum results in high
levels of pollution, according to Martin. Martin is a *Mother
Earth News* contributing editor.

As you read, consider the following questions:

1. According to Martin, how much municipal waste does
   the United States dispose of each year?
2. In the author's view, what is the main problem with
   landfills?
3. What is the weakest link in the recycling loop, in the
   author's opinion?

To understand the national obsession with saving our garbage we have only to look to the pages of the *Seguin Gazette*, a newspaper in South Texas. "Nothing is junk—save all scrap metal so it can be recycled," a reporter urges. "In multicar families use only one car . . . and take up walking. [Do] your grocery shopping twice a week instead of every day, and if you live close to the market area walk and take your own basket." The story would read like a how-to brochure on environmentally sustainable living in the 21st century—if it weren't an announcement for the War Effort, circa 1942.

During World War II the fact that saving empty toothpaste tubes would keep the country's water and air clean wasn't of imminent concern. Recycling for the war was simple: Save now, have a better world to live in later. Sixty years later, has the message changed so much?

The Battle of the Bulge

It's no secret that the United States is the most wasteful country on the planet. We dispose of 210 million tons of municipal waste every year, and the yearly costs of that disposal is just shy of $45 billion. Combine residential and business garbage with the truckloads of industrial waste produced in the U.S. and we have an annual pile of trash weighing 12 billion tons. Not surprisingly, what we do with our detritus has become a war of its own.

America's most recent wake-up call to the mess it was making came in 1987, when a trash barge called the Mobro 4000 motored up and down the Eastern seaboard looking for a landfill in which to dump 3,200 tons of New York State's garbage. During thousands of miles of fruitless wandering (the Mobro eventually returned to port, still fully loaded), trash became a headline attraction in newspapers and television stations all over the country.

While waste was news, each story prompted more and more people to question the ethics behind throwing away so much at one time. In 1988, the Environmental Protection Agency (EPA) took the issue seriously enough to recommend that 25% of municipal trash be recycled by the end of a five-year program.

Twelve years of good effort, endless debates and considerable expense have actually made a difference. As of 1995 27% of the country's waste was recycled (compared to 6.3% in 1960), and projected numbers for this year report Americans reusing 30% to 35% with recovery rates for paper exceeding 45%.

Nonetheless, what does recycling do for us on a day-to-day basis? It certainly keeps us busy. We set up elaborate sorting systems in our homes—with glass in one bin and paper in the next, rinsing here and bundling there upon penalty of fines or worse: missing the pickup date! And what about the fact that recycling itself is a dirty business, with loud collection trucks plying the predawn streets? It's expensive, as is normal waste disposal, and in increasingly mandatory fashion our taxes are used to pay for an industry that struggles to turn a profit. Is recycling worth it?

Dr. Alan Hershkowitz, director of the National Resources Defense Council, thinks it is. "Everything costs money," he cautions, "including incinerators and landfills." The difference, he explains, is that recycling is designed to ease the impact we have on our environments and alleviate the burden our waste has on our communities. "So yes," Hershkowitz says, "it is worth it."

Since tax money is at the root of any waste solution, the question remains: How can we use the money to deal with our waste most effectively, decrease risks to human health, and foster a healthy environment to live in? It seems that, compared to landfilling, recycling is the economic and environmental favorite by a long shot.

Closing the Loop on Landfills

If done right, landfills can be a viable disposal option. If done wrong, they can be an environmental and economic disaster.

The main problem with landfills is that they are complicated structures that are difficult to maintain. Of particular concern is the wastewater created inside landfills as leachate. In order to keep the toxic material from leaking into the local drinking water, these football stadium-sized holes require a combination of liners made from clay, high-density polyethylene (HDPE) plastic or composite membranes. But according to the Environmental Research Foundation in Annapolis, Maryland, clay will dry and crack over time, HDPE will degrade with household chemicals, and composite liners made from clay and plastic will leak somewhere between 0.2 and 10 gallons a day after ten years. Even with complex leachate collection plumbing built into landfills, none of these solutions is 100% foolproof (collection pipes tend to clog and back up).

Trash Leaders

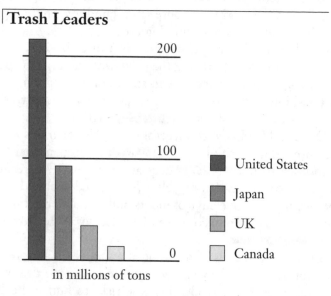

in millions of tons

Sam Martin, *Mother Earth News*, December/January 2001.

"The EPA technicians that currently oversee landfill design and regulation have said that their own engineering standards would not last," warns Will Ferretti, executive director of the National Recycling Coalition. "They're saying that they could break down in a 30-year time frame. It's clearly a concern and we have asked the EPA to revisit their regulations in that light."

Leaving a Smaller Footprint

To be fair, however, recycling doesn't clear every environmental hurdle either. Products remade from recycled waste such as paper and plastic go through a chemical process. In the case of newsprint, there are a dozen or so supposedly

negative

nonhazardous chemicals used in the remanufacturing process, including a water/hydrogen peroxide solution to remove ink from the used paper. Paper recycling also uses thousands of gallons of water.

Compared to making paper from virgin materials, however, recycling is clearly more responsible to the environment. In addition to the hundreds of highly toxic chemicals used in papermaking such as chlorine, dioxin and furan, consider what it takes to harvest a forest, build logging roads, and cut and haul trees. The paper recycling industry alone saves 17 trees for every ton of paper it keeps out of the landfill. In 1996 America recovered 42.3 million tons of paper, saving more than 719 million trees.

The plastic manufacturing industry provides an even more compelling case for re-use. According to Hershkowitz, the production of plastics from crude petroleum causes "some of the most substantial public health threats" of any manufacturing process. Indeed, in 1994 U.S. plastic production was responsible for 111 million pounds of toxic air emissions and 12 million pounds of ozone-depleting chemicals.

"You have to ask which activity leaves a smaller footprint on the environment," says Ferretti when comparing recycling to landfilling. "Recycling relies on industrial activity to function, and industrial activity, by nature, has byproducts that can affect the environment. But from a life cycle standpoint, recycling is much more preferable [to landfills] because it has the least impact."

Consequently, the amount of landfills in the U.S. has decreased from 8,000 in 1988 to just over 3,000 in 1996.

Growing Acceptance

The "reuse and recycle" solution is not a new idea; it has, however, long been recognized as the most economically savvy one. Corporations and big industry such as Ford Motor Co., Herman Miller Furniture and Interface Carpets have been doing it for years because they save millions of dollars by cutting back on production costs. If the numbers don't prove recycling's worth, then common sense does.

"Certainly there is a segment of the population that believes that they have a God-given right to just use stuff up and throw it away," offers Ferretti. "But I don't think that segment of the population will always exist."

The statistics overwhelmingly support his prediction. The most recent EPA statistics (1997) reported that curbside pickup was available in over 49 states and 8,000 cities (Hawaii has since joined the team), and the National Recycling Coalition has estimated that around 84% of the population now has access to a recycling facility. As a result, the amount of municipal waste that has been recycled in the last decade has nearly doubled. By all accounts—public opinion polls and government studies included—people seem to want to recycle.

Of course, they also have to recycle. Fines and penalties for ignoring recycling laws are stiff, and this Big Brother finger-wagging is part of what prompted John Tierney, a *New York Times* reporter, to write his scathing rebuttal of the whole philosophy in 1996. Entitled "Recycling is Garbage," Tierney's article asserts that the resources, labor and sum personal time involved in recycling far outweigh any environmental or economic benefit. He further suggests that we not only have plenty of landfill space, but that landfills are an economic boon to the communities surrounding them. Tierney's engaging style was an instant hit among antirecycling political activists, but his often curious interpretation of facts left many scientists puzzled.

Recycling's Hurdle

"Nothing is perfectly efficient," says Hershkowitz, "and no one I know of is seriously suggesting 100% recovery for recycling. Still, the main roadblock to increased levels of recycling is the absence of a commitment to this issue by industries that have many economic incentives not to recycle or use recycled materials."

Which brings us to a problem in the recycling industry: consumer support. Widely considered the weakest link in the recycling loop, recycled product sales are not what they should be—either because recycled products are more expensive or because they're unavailable. For that reason, the recycling industry isn't getting the financial support it needs to compete with the federally subsidized incentives to which

Hershkowitz refers. Most people simply don't realize that they have the option to buy recycled.

"Aluminum, steel and glass are under our noses, and they're not marked like paper usually is," explains George Rutherford of America Recycles Day. "But aluminum, steel and glass have a 30% to 40% recycled content. Plastic doesn't. It's by and large a virgin product. Also, cars are one of the most widely recycled products we have."

Nevertheless, the enormous enthusiasm for recycling programs suggests that there are plenty of reasons to recycle other than being able to buy more stuff, remanufactured or not.

"Recycling is one of those few activities that [allows us] to make a direct connection between our behaviors and some kind of contribution to a quality of life that is hard to find out there," explains Ferretti. "Maybe altruistic is the right word, but I think there's something more innate and more satisfying that is occurring. I would argue that the quality of life both now and for your children and grandchildren is enhanced by that rather modest and mundane action of separating out some portion of our waste and putting it out at the curb for recycling."

While human nature is oftentimes up for speculation, the fact that recycling is the best solution for waste disposal isn't. The evidence and the desire have never been more telling.

> "*Misleading educational programs encourage the waste of resources when they overstate the benefits of recycling.*"

The Benefits of Recycling Are Exaggerated

Daniel K. Benjamin

Common misconceptions have led to an exaggeration of recycling's benefits, claims Daniel K. Benjamin in the following viewpoint. Contrary to popular belief, he argues, the United States has more landfill capacity than ever before, and modern landfills pose little risk to people or the environment. Moreover, industries have come up with more environmentally-friendly production methods, and the quantity of American waste is shrinking, Benjamin asserts. He maintains that the recycling process actually poses a threat to the environment. Benjamin, an economics professor at Clemson University, is an associate of the Property and Environment Research Center, a free-market environmental policy think tank.

As you read, consider the following questions:

1. In Benjamin's opinion, how do modern landfills eliminate the potential for environmental problems?
2. What examples of human innovation continue to increase America's resources, in the author's view?
3. According to the author, in what unexpected ways does the pollution associated with recycling show up?

Governments on both shores of the Atlantic and both coasts of America have recently announced plans to force businesses and individuals to recycle more trash. The European Union has ordered the citizens of the United Kingdom to roughly double their recycling rates by 2008, while the city governments of New York and Seattle have proposed mandatory expansions of existing recycling programs.

These moves are not based on new developments in resource conservation; instead they—like other mandatory recycling programs—rest on misconceptions of mythic proportions. This essay discusses the most egregious of these myths.

Myth 1: Our Garbage Will Bury Us

Since the 1980s, people repeatedly have claimed that the United States faces a landfill crisis. Former Vice President Al Gore, for example, asserted we are "running out of ways to dispose of our waste in a manner that keeps it out of either sight or mind."

This claim originated in the 1980s, when the waste disposal industry moved to using fewer but much larger landfills. The Environmental Protection Agency, the press, and other commentators focused on the falling number of landfills, rather than on their growing overall capacity, and concluded that we were running out of space. The EPA also underestimated the prospects for creating additional capacity.

In fact, the United States today has more landfill capacity than ever before. In 2001, the nation's landfills could accommodate 18 years' worth of rubbish, an amount 25 percent greater than a decade before. To be sure, there are a few places where capacity has shrunk. But the uneven distribution of available landfill space is no more important than is the uneven distribution of auto manufacturing: Trash is an interstate business, with 47 states exporting the stuff and 45 importing it. Indeed, the total land area needed to hold all of America's garbage for the next century would be only about 10 miles square.

Myth 2: Our Garbage Will Poison Us

The claim that our trash might poison us is impossible to completely refute, because almost anything might pose a threat. But the EPA itself acknowledges that the risks to humans (and presumably plants and animals) from modern landfills are virtually nonexistent: Modern landfills can be expected to cause 5.7 cancer-related deaths over the next 300 years—one every 50 years. To put this in perspective, cancer kills over 560,000 people every year in the United States.

Older landfills do possess a potential for harm to the ecosystem and to humans, especially when built on wetlands (or swamps), because pollutants can leach from them. When located on dry land, however, even old-style landfills generally pose minimal danger, in part because remarkably little biodegradation takes place in them.

Modern landfills eliminate essentially any potential for problems. Siting occurs away from groundwater supplies, and the landfills are built on a foundation of several feet of dense clay, covered with thick plastic liners. This layer is covered by several feet of gravel or sand. Any leachate is drained out via collection pipes and sent to municipal wastewater plants for treatment. Methane gas produced by biodegradation is drawn off by wells on site and burned or purified and sold.

Myth 3: Packaging Is Our Problem

Contrary to current wisdom, packaging can reduce total rubbish produced. The average household in the United States generates one third less trash each year than does the average household in Mexico, partly because packaging reduces breakage and food waste. Turning a live chicken into a meal creates food waste. When chickens are processed commercially, the waste goes into marketable products (such as pet food), instead of into a landfill. Commercial processing of 1,000 chickens requires about 17 pounds of packaging, but it also recycles at least 2,000 pounds of by-products.

The gains from packaging have been growing over time, because companies have been reducing the weight of the packages they use. During the late 1970s and 1980s, although the number of packages entering landfills rose substantially, the total weight of those discards declined by 40 percent. Over the past 25 years the weights of individual packages have been reduced by amounts ranging from 30 percent (2-liter soft drink bottles) to 70 percent (plastic gro-

Packaging Slims Down

Plastic grocery sack, thickness
1976	⟶	2001
2.3 mils		0.7 mils

Plastic fruit sack, thickness
1970	⟶	2001
1.05 mils		0.5 mils

Plastic trash bag, thickness
1975	⟶	2001
2.5–3.0 mils		1.0–1.25 mils

PET 2-liter bottle, weight
1978	⟶	2002
68 grams		48 grams

HDPE milk jug, weight
1965	⟶	1990
120 grams		65 grams

Aluminum can, weight
1972	⟶	2002
20.8 grams		13.7 grams

Consumer's Research, November 2003.

cery sacks and trash bags). Even aluminum beverage cans weigh 40 percent less than they used to.

Myth 4: We Must Achieve Trash Independence

Numerous commentators contend that each state should achieve "trash independence" by disposing within its borders all of its rubbish. But, as with all voluntary trade, interstate trade in trash raises our wealth as a nation, perhaps by as much as $4 billion. Most of the increased wealth accrues to the citizens of areas importing trash.

Not only is the potential threat posed by modern landfills negligible, but transporting rubbish across state lines has no effect on the environmental impact of its disposal. Moving a ton of trash by truck is no more hazardous than moving a ton of any other commodity.

Myth 5: We Squander Irreplaceable Resources When We Do Not Recycle

In fact, available stocks of most natural resources are growing rather than shrinking, but the reason is not recycling.

Market prices are the best measure of natural resource scarcity. Rising prices imply that a resource is getting more scarce. Falling prices imply that it is becoming more plentiful. Applying this measure to oil, we find that over the past 125 years, oil has become no more scarce, despite our growing use of it. Reserves of other fossil fuels as well as other natural resources are also growing.

Thanks to innovation, we now produce about twice as much output per unit of energy as we did 50 years ago and five times as much as we did 200 years ago. Optical fiber carries 625 times more calls than the copper wire of 20 years ago, bridges are built with less steel, and automobile and truck engines consume less fuel per unit of work performed. The list goes on and on. Human innovation continues to increase the amount of resources at our command.

Myth 6: Recycling Always Protects the Environment

Recycling is a manufacturing process with environmental impacts. Viewed across a wide spectrum of goods, recycling sometimes cuts pollution, but not always. The EPA has examined both virgin paper processing and recycled paper processing for toxic substances and found that toxins often are more prevalent in the recycling processes.

Often the pollution associated with recycling shows up in unexpected ways. Curbside recycling, for example, requires that more trucks be used to collect the same amount of waste materials. Thus, Los Angeles has 800 rubbish trucks rather than 400, because of its curb-side recycling. This means more iron ore and coal mining, steel and rubber manufacturing, petroleum extraction and refining—and of course extra air pollution in the Los Angeles basin.

Myth 7: Recycling Saves Resources

It is widely claimed that recycling "saves resources." Proponents usually focus on savings of a specific resource, or they single out particularly successful examples such as the recycling of aluminum cans.

But using less of one resource generally means using more of other resources. Franklin Associates, a firm that consults on behalf of the EPA, has compared the costs per ton of handling rubbish through three methods: disposal into landfills (but with a voluntary drop-off or buy-back recycling program), a baseline curbside recycling program, and an extensive curbside recycling program.

On average, extensive recycling is 35 percent more costly than conventional disposal, and basic curbside recycling is 55 percent more costly than conventional disposal. That is, curbside recycling uses far more resources. As one expert puts it, adding curbside recycling is "like moving from once-a-week garbage collection to twice a week."

Myth 8: Without Forced Recycling Mandates, There Would Not Be Recycling

This view reflects ignorance about the extent of recycling in the private sector, which is as old as trash itself. Scavenging may, in fact, be the oldest profession. In the 19th century, people bid for the right to scavenge New York City's rubbish, and Winslow Homer's 1859 etching, *Scene on the Back Bay Lands*, reveals adults and children digging through the detritus of the Boston city dump. Rag dealers were a constant of American life until driven out of business by the federal Wool Products Labeling Act of 1939, which stigmatized products made of recycled wool and cotton. And long before state or local governments had even contemplated the word recycling, makers of steel, aluminum, and many other products were recycling manufacturing scraps, and some were even operating post-consumer drop-off centers.

Recycling is a long-practiced, productive, indeed essential, element of the market system. Informed, voluntary recycling conserves resources and raises our wealth. In sharp contrast, misleading educational programs encourage the waste of resources when they overstate the benefits of recycling. And mandatory recycling programs, in which people are compelled to do what they know is not sensible, routinely make society worse off. Market prices are sufficient to induce the trashman to come, and to make his burden bearable, and neither he nor we can hope for any better than that.

3

> *"The best thing we can do is to ensure prospective vehicle purchasers are educated . . . and encourage them to make the most environmentally sound decisions."*

People Should Be Discouraged from Buying Polluting Sport-Utility Vehicles

Friends of the Earth

Consumers should be made aware that sport-utility vehicles (SUVs) pollute more than passenger vehicles do, claims Friends of the Earth in the following viewpoint. Because SUVs are considered trucks and not passenger cars, they are not subject to strict fuel economy regulations; as a result, they emit more of the carbon dioxide emissions that contribute to global warming, the author maintains. SUVs also emit higher levels of other pollutants such as carbon monoxide, hydrocarbons, and nitrogen oxides, the author asserts. Friends of the Earth is a grassroots organization that supports environmental and social justice.

As you read, consider the following questions:
1. According to Friends of the Earth, what fuel economy standards must light trucks meet?
2. In the author's view, what will choosing a vehicle that gets twenty-five rather than twenty miles per gallon prevent?
3. What could automakers do to improve the fuel efficiency of SUVs, in the author's opinion?

SUVs represent a paradox to consumers—television advertisements present them as a way to return to nature, yet they actually accelerate existing environmental problems. Commercials often depict happy families driving on mountain roads, avoiding falling rocks and enjoying the flowered wilderness in leather-seated comfort. The sad truth is that these vehicles are contributing to the destruction of our natural resources.

What Is Wrong with SUVs?

In reality, only 5 percent of SUVs are ever taken off-road, and the vast majority of these vehicles are used for everyday driving. And there are a lot of them on the roads. In 1985, SUVs accounted for only 2 percent of new vehicle sales. SUVs now account for one in four new vehicles sold, and sales continue to climb.

Driving an SUV has a much greater impact on the environment than driving other passenger cars. In large part, this is due to double standards set by law and government regulations. For example, current federal regulations allow SUVs to have far worse fuel economy than other vehicles. The federal corporate average fuel economy (CAFE) standards set the fuel economy goals for new passenger cars at 27.5 miles per gallon (mpg). But under the law, SUVs are not considered cars—they are characterized as light trucks. Light trucks only have to achieve 20.7 mpg. It should be noted that this is an average for all light trucks, which is why it is possible to have SUVs on the road that only achieve 12 mpg. In fact, some SUVs, like the massive Ford Excursion, are so large that they no longer qualify as "light trucks," and are not subject to any kind of fuel economy standards.

When CAFE was instituted in the 1970s, there were few SUVs and light trucks on the road, and they were primarily used for farm and commercial work. Today, however, the demographics of an SUV buyer are quite different. The amount of gasoline burned by a vehicle is important for several reasons. The most crucial is the threat of global warming.

Contrary to some rhetoric you may have heard, global warming has been extremely well studied. In 2001, the Intergovernmental Panel on Climate Change (IPCC) issued a report on global warming with many dire predictions. The World Meteorological Organization and the United Nations Environment Programme created the IPCC in 1988 to study the risks associated with global climate change. The IPCC found that about three quarters of the anthropogenic (caused by humans) emissions of carbon dioxide to the atmosphere during the past 20 years is due to fossil fuel burning. The IPCC anticipates higher temperatures and heat waves over the next century, as well as more intense and dangerous storms.

The EPA seconds these concerns. According to the EPA, "increasing concentrations of greenhouse gases are likely to accelerate the rate of climate change. Scientists expect that the average global surface temperature could rise 1–4.5°F (0.6–2.5°C) in the next fifty years, and 2.2–10°F (1.4–5.8°C) in the next century, with significant regional variation. Evaporation will increase as the climate warms, which will increase average global precipitation. Soil moisture is likely to decline in many regions, and intense rainstorms are likely to become more frequent. Sea level is likely to rise two feet along most of the U.S. coast."

The Importance of Fuel Economy

According to the U.S. Environmental Protection Agency (EPA), one of the most important things you can do to reduce global warming pollution is to buy a vehicle with higher fuel economy. This is because every gallon of gasoline your vehicle burns puts 20 pounds of carbon dioxide (CO_2) into the atmosphere. Scientific evidence strongly suggests that the rapid buildup of CO_2 and other greenhouse gases in the atmosphere is raising the earth's temperature and changing the earth's climate with potentially serious consequences. Choosing a vehicle that gets 25 rather than 20 miles per gallon will prevent 10 tons of CO_2 from being released over the lifetime of your vehicle. Passenger cars and trucks account for about 20 percent of all U.S. CO_2 emissions.

Today a car that gets approximately 27.5 mpg, like a Volkswagen New Beetle, will emit 54 tons of carbon dioxide (CO_2) from the burning of gasoline over its lifetime. An SUV that gets 14 mpg, like a Lincoln Navigator, will emit over 100 tons of CO_2 over its lifetime. A *Harper's Magazine* writer took the massive Ford Excursion, the biggest of all SUVs for a test drive. During a drive around a city, the mighty Excursion was only getting 3.7 miles per gallon. It is estimated the Excursion will produce 134 tons of carbon dioxide during its lifetime. The National Academy of Sciences estimates that if fuel economy had not been improved in the late 1970s, U.S. fuel consumption would be about 2.8 million barrels of oil per day higher than it is. This is about 14 percent of today's oil consumption. However, all of the major fleet-wide improvements in vehicle fuel economy occurred from the middle 1970s through the late 1980s, but it has been consistently falling since then. In fact, average new vehicle fuel economy fell in 2000 to 24 mpg, its lowest level in 20 years. The increasing market share of light trucks and SUVs accounts for much of the decline in fuel economy of the overall new light vehicle fleet.

Global warming is a real danger that cannot be ignored. However, automakers continue to build fuel-inefficient vehicles. The vehicles we drive are contributing to this problem, but automakers don't seem particularly concerned. . . .

The SUV's Smog-Forming Emissions

SUVs have a significant environmental impact even beyond the problem of global warming. Federal law gives heavy sport utility vehicles permission to emit higher levels of toxic and noxious pollution—carbon monoxide, hydrocarbons, and nitrogen oxides.

Sport utility vehicles can spew 30 percent more carbon monoxide and hydrocarbons and 75 percent more nitrogen oxides than passenger cars. These combustion pollutants contribute to eye and throat irritation, coughing, nausea, dizziness, fatigue, confusion and headaches. Hydrocarbons and nitrogen oxides are precursors to ground level ozone, which causes asthma and lung damage.

These pollutants are regulated under the Clean Air Act of 1990. If a region is unable to reduce their emissions for these pollutants, the EPA may impose penalties. This is known as reaching "attainment." Many of the large urban areas in the U.S. are in "serious nonattainment."

The U.S. EPA and the Department of Energy have teamed up to create a website that lists vehicles' fuel economy, and compares vehicles to each other. It also goes a step further by giving each vehicle a score of zero to ten for the amount of smog producing pollution the vehicle emits. Ten is considered a perfect score. Unfortunately, many popular SUVs only rate four or below, with many at zero. This rating system is an excellent tool to help people see the impact of their vehicle choice, and it is a great help for people interested in purchasing a new vehicle. [Table 1] looks at the fuel economy and emissions scores of some of the most popular 4-wheel drive SUVs. All data is from the U.S. EPA and the Department of Energy. . . .

Table 1: Rating SUVs

Manufacturer	Model	Cylinder	Liter	City MPG	Hwy MPG	EPA Rating
Dodge	Durango	8	5.2	12	17	1
Ford	Expedition	8	5.4	12	17	1
Jeep	Grand Cherokee	6	4.0	15	20	4
GMC	Yukon	8	5.7	14	16	0
Lincoln	Navigator	8	5.4	12	16	1
Land Rover	Range Rover	8	4.6	12	15	1
Chevrolet	Suburban	8	5.3	14	16	0

Friends of the Earth, "What Is Wrong with SUVs?" www.suv.org/environ. html.

The Impact of SUVs on Air Quality

Unfortunately, increasing numbers of Americans are living in areas with poor air quality from ozone pollution, according to the American Lung Association (ALP). The ALA found that 141 million Americans lived in areas with poor air quality during 1997–1999. This is nine million more people than in the previous two-year period.

The Washington, D.C., region has a non-attainment ranking of serious for ozone pollution. As mentioned above, ground level ozone can be a serious problem for many areas. When a region has a "bad air day," it is usually because the levels of ozone in the air have created an unhealthy situation.

In the case of Washington, D.C., the EPA is considering cutting off the region's road building funds until the region can come up with a viable solution to the pollution problem. However, standing in the way of any solution is the number of SUVs on the road.

The amount of nitrogen oxide in the D.C. region's air [was] expected to be eight tons per day over the limit of 162 tons by 2005, according to Ronald Kirby of the Metropolitan Washington Council of Governments. In July [2001], Mr. Kirby told the *Washington Post* that the growth of SUVs on the roads in the past few years has been tremendous, jumping from 15 percent of all vehicles to 25 percent in just three years. In fact, Marsha Kaiser, planning director for the Maryland Department of Transportation, said that her agency predicts the "huge increase" in SUVs on the road will tip the region beyond its limits. All passenger vehicles pollute, but SUVs produce so much more pollution than the average car. In terms of air pollution, one SUV is like two or three cars on the road.

This is a very significant development, and it shows the kind of impact that a large amount of polluting SUVs can have on air quality. The Fairfax County government, in Northern Virginia, is concerned enough about this problem to halt purchases of SUVs for official business and replace some of the ones they already own. This step is "more than just symbolic," according to County Supervisor Gerald Connolly, who believes the county needs to change how it approaches car purchases.

Many regions still haven't gotten the message, however. Governors attending the National Governors Association meeting in Rhode Island in August 2001 drove SUVs provided free of charge by General Motors. Sixty-five GMC Yukons were shipped up to Rhode Island for the event. Governor Lincoln Almond said the state was appreciative. "We don't take a gesture by GM and tell them what to do," he said. According to the U.S. EPA, various models of the Yukon get between 12 and 17 miles per gallon, and most receive a zero out of ten on the pollution scale. . . .

In July 2001, the National Academy of Sciences (NAS) released a study on fuel economy standards. The NAS found that light trucks, SUVs, minivans, and pickup trucks could reach 28–30 mpg for an additional cost of $1,200–$1,300. Automakers make an average of $10,000 in pure profit on each SUV sold. It shouldn't be too much to ask automakers to sacrifice a small amount of their profits to clean up these vehicles. The NAS study specifically pointed out that safety would not be sacrificed, and actually assumes an increase in vehicle weight, which is associated with certain safety-enhancing features. However, the NAS points out that reducing the weight of the largest SUVs on the roads would make all drivers safer, since the biggest SUVs tend to do the most damage in an accident. . . .

We may wish people who don't need giant vehicles won't buy them, but people will buy whatever they want. The best thing we can do is to ensure prospective vehicle purchasers are educated on their choices, and encourage them to make the most environmentally sound decisions.

The good news is that SUVs can be improved without much effort, and without sacrificing safety. Automakers have made some baby steps, but they have so far been unwilling to make a serious effort to improve these vehicles.

In the meantime, we must work to change the federal standards governing these vehicles. SUV drivers are not to blame for the lower fuel economy and emissions standards that these vehicles enjoy, and SUV drivers are not to blame for automaker's lack of innovation and improvement. Automakers have shown a strong unwillingness over the years to clean up their products, or even to make them safer without a push from the federal government—or from consumers. Therefore, people who are concerned about these issues must work to educate the public while working to improve the federal regulations governing SUVs. Only education and improved environmental standards will push automakers into cleaning up these vehicles.

In 2000, Ford Motor Company announced plans to improve their SUV fleet fuel economy by 25 percent by 2005. This is a great first step, and it shows that automakers are capable of improving their vehicles. It also shows that a concerned public can influence a company like Ford. This is why educated consumers must demand better vehicles, and demand that Congress and the president finally address the problem with today's fuel economy standards.

But automakers are unlikely to make significant improvements unless they are pushed. William Clay Ford, the chairman of Ford Motor Company, put it best. "The best way to get the auto industry to stop dragging its feet is to have us race against each other. We love to do that, and we're good at it." The race will begin as soon as fuel economy standards are improved to a realistic level.

| "*New SUVs . . . are a far sight more [environmentally] responsible than the 15 million used cars that become obsolete each year.*"

Claims Against Sport-Utility Vehicles Are Unwarranted

Nick Gillespie

Claims against sport-utility vehicles (SUVs) are unfounded, argues Nick Gillespie in the following viewpoint. SUVs actually pollute less than do older vehicles that met emissions standards in the 1980s when they were produced, he claims. In fact all cars and light trucks, including SUVs, account for only 1.5 percent of global greenhouse gases each year, he maintains. Gillespie is editor in chief of *Reason* magazine.

As you read, consider the following questions:
1. In Gillespie's view, what should be done to target gross polluters?
2. What possibility is ignored by people who believe that SUVs increase dependence on foreign oil, in the author's opinion?
3. What does the author contend is the symbolic attack on the SUV?

M uch of the animus against the SUV [sport-utility vehi-
cle] takes the form of standard-issue environmental
concerns—they are gas guzzlers!—and what might be called
automotive McCarthyism—they are unpatriotic! Increasingly, though, SUVs are coming in for abuse on the symbolic level, for what they purportedly reveal about the sorry,
fallen state of the American soul. SUVs . . . are "the very emblem of contemporary selfishness." The first two criticisms
don't pack as much horsepower as they seem to at first; the
last is interesting mostly because it participates in the
centuries-old tradition of demonizing consumption choices
not merely as mistaken but morally deranged and leading to
the destabilization of decent society.

The Myth of the Gas Guzzling SUV

While it's true that new SUVs get rotten gas mileage compared to new cars, it's equally true that they match up pretty
well against the older cars that do most of the real polluting.
As Hans Eisenbeis wrote in *Reason* [in 2002], "New SUVs
. . . are a far sight more [environmentally] responsible than
the 15 million used cars that become obsolete each year.
Even the greenest autos built in the 1980s, for example, are
90 percent dirtier and less efficient than new SUVs." As relevant, emissions from all cars and light trucks (a category
that includes SUVs, minivans, and pickup trucks) account
for just 1.5 percent of all global greenhouse gases annually.

Hence, as Jacob Sullum has suggested, even completely
getting rid of all cars and light trucks is not going to massively
alter the global environment (which keeps getting better and
better anyway; even Southern California, the legendary
Kingdom of Smog, is setting records for air quality). And if
someone really wants to target gross polluters, he would do
well to focus less on broad classes of automobiles and more
on individual vehicles, since 5 percent to 10 percent of vehicles account for about half of all tailpipe emissions in the U.S.
If you want to clean the air, dither less over what Jesus would
drive and fund a jalopy buyback program instead.

Are SUVs—often derided as a cartoon version of the grand
old American land yacht—unpatriotic? Do they, as a series of
controversial, semi-serious TV commercials, funnel oil-

stained dollars directly into the hands of Middle Eastern terrorists? If this tortured logic is to be taken seriously, then there's plenty of blame to go around. More precisely, everyone who buys gas, oil, Vaseline, and other petroleum products is one-quarter as guilty as Mohammed Atta for [the September 11, 2001, terrorist attacks]. After all, according to the Department of Energy, in 2001, Persian Gulf states accounted for about 25 percent of net oil imports, as calculated in barrels per year.

Varvel. © 2004 by Creators Syndicate. Reproduced by permission.

Those pushing the "Do you now or have you ever driven a car that gets less than 27 miles per gallon?" line stress the need to end America's dependence on nefarious "foreign oil." Yet no one in that crowd . . . seems the slightest bit interested in ramping up domestic oil production. Which suggests that, in this case anyway, patriotism is simply the last refuge to which an environmentalist clings.

The Symbolic Attack

If neither the environmentalist nor the nativist condemnation quite drives the anti-SUV argument across the finish line, there's still the symbolic attack. In a review of Keith

Bradsher's new book, *High and Mighty*—which is poised to become the Bible of the anti-SUV crowd—[Brookings Institute scholar] Gregg Easterbrook makes it clear that these popular vehicles are nothing less than pure evil. Indeed, they are "sociopathic cars" and "anti-social automobiles" that create "the very emblem of contemporary selfishness." Along with a generally fascinating recounting of . . . how federal industrial policy (as played out most clearly in the tax code) has effected automotive design, Easterbrook rehearses versions of the other two arguments, writing that SUVs "emit far more smog-forming pollutants and greenhouse gases than regular cars" and that they "keep American society perilously dependent on Persian Gulf Oil."

He also writes that contrary to common perception, that SUVs are unsafe, both for their passengers and other motorists. Respectable researchers differ on that point, but Easterbrook also throws in a class-based caveat that recalls recurrent aristocratic fears of the lower orders rising up against their betters. "As the first generation of monster SUVs gets traded in," he frets, "these behemoths will begin entering the used-car market, where they will be purchased by immigrants, the lower middle class, and the poor, who generally speed, run lights, drive drunk, and crash more often than the prosperous classes. . . . This segment of the population is about to be armed with three-ton SUVs and enormous pickups." In the true spirit of noblesse oblige, however, Easterbrook doesn't argue that the huddled masses should have their driving privileges revoked. Instead, he implies that the vehicles beyond their weak impulse control should be barred from the mean streets of America. "Since when," he asks, "is there a 'right' to imperil others? . . . Driving an SUV or a light pickup is a public act that creates avoidable public risk."

Yet despite his nods to the environmental, nativist, and safety debates, Easterbrook ultimately seems more interested in what he calls the "existential fiasco of the SUV." The SUV isn't a response to "road rage" but rather a "cause" of that dubious but newsworthy social problem. Automakers market "hostility" via menacing SUV grills and are "guilty of advancing the fiction that SUVs are intended for offroad adventures." Curiously, customers don't seem to be in on the con; rather, they're simply passive dupes of such a "romantic deception," not willing participants. "There are lots of self-centered and self-absorbed people with little interest in their neighbors," declares Easterbrook. "Somebody finally made a class of vehicles to bring out the worst in them."

Is there any way out of the SUV crisis? Or will America slowly be taken over by driving machines that are slowly re-programming us all—even the poor and the foreign-born!—into increasingly hostile drivers and bad citizens of some coming Road Warrior republic?

This is an age of terror and preventive war; perhaps it's time we start preemptively arresting the domestic terrorists hiding behind the darkened windshields of SUVs. If Easterbrook is right that SUVs declare of their drivers, "I have serious psychological problems," maybe Attorney General John Ashcroft can find room for such subversives at Camp Gitmo[1] or some other laboratory of democracy.

1. Gitmo is short for the U.S. Naval Station at Guantánamo Bay, Cuba, where those captured in the war on terror are being detained.

Periodical Bibliography

The following articles have been selected to supplement the diverse views presented in this chapter.

Daniel Brook — "The Ongoing Tragedy of the Commons," *Social Science Journal*, October 2001.

Patrick Burnson — "Stupid, Ugly, Vulgar," *World Trade*, April 2003.

George W. Crabtree, Mildred S. Dresselhaus, and Michelle V. Buchanan — "The Hydrogen Economy," *Physics Today*, December 2004.

Gregg Easterbrook — "Axle of Evil—America's Twisted Love Affair with Sociopathic Cars," *New Republic*, January 20, 2003.

Environment — "Sport Inefficiency," December 2001.

Jim Fulton — "Get Rolling with Hybrid Vehicles," *Detroit Free Press*, January 15, 2004.

Jerome Goldstein — "Enlarging the Impact of an Industry," *Biocycle*, July 2000.

Donald L. Guertin — "A Daunting Challenge: Meeting Human Needs While Managing Carbon Emissions," *Chemistry and Industry*, December 3, 2001.

Thomas Q. Hogye — "Acting Responsibly: Genuine Recyclers Have a Duty to Recover Resources Safely and Responsibly," *Recycling Today*, December 2004.

Dwight R. Lee — "Getting the Most Out of Pollution," *Freeman: Ideas on Liberty*, October 2001.

Jim Motavalli — "Recycling's Great Leap Forward," *E Magazine*, March 2001.

Keith Naughton — "The Unstoppable SUV," *Newsweek*, July 2, 2001.

Matthew Power — "The Trash Folder: As Waste, Our Computers Are Not So Easily Erased," *Harper's*, January 2003.

Rolf Priesnitz — "Stop Driving Yourself to Extinction," *Natural Life*, March/April 2004.

Ed Ring — "Hydrogen Fuel Cell Cars," *EcoWorld*, December 4, 2000.

Greg Schneider — "Priming the Public For Hydrogen Fuel," *Washington Post*, November 10, 2004.

Gary Witzenburg — "How Viable Are HEVs, Really?" *Automotive Industries*, March 2004.

CHAPTER 4

What Government Policies Would Reduce Pollution?

Chapter Preface

Today's cruise ships are like floating cities. *Voyager of the Seas*, one of the world's largest cruise ships, is 1,017 feet in length and carries more than five thousand passengers and crew. *Voyager* boasts five dining areas, seven bars, a conference center, three swimming pools, a 1,350-person theater, and a variety of stores and entertainment facilities. Not unlike a small city, *Voyager* also produces daily waste and pollutants, including as much as thirty-seven thousand gallons of oily bilge water, thirty thousand gallons of sewage, and 250,000 gallons of non-sewage wastewater from showers, sinks, laundries, baths, and galleys. In addition, such a vessel can generate tons of garbage, solid waste, and toxic chemicals.

What concerns some analysts about cruise ships is that they clearly produce as much waste as a small U.S. city, but they are not subject to the same regulations. According to the Ocean Conservancy, "Under the Clean Water Act, cities must treat their wastes, limit the amount of pollution they discharge, and monitor and report on discharges from sewage treatment facilities. Yet cruise ships are not required to obtain Clean Water Act discharge permits, nor to monitor or report on their discharges. Gray water from on-board laundries, galleys, baths, and showers is essentially unregulated." While ocean and coastal conservation activists argue that Congress should pass laws that specifically regulate cruise ship waste, the cruise ship industry maintains that it can effectively regulate itself. This debate illustrates how difficult it is to define the role that government should play in reducing pollution.

The cruise ship industry claims that strict laws to regulate ship waste are unnecessary because the industry has voluntarily established strict practices and procedures that mirror or exceed current laws that regulate ships in U.S. waters. The industry argues that failure to observe strict waste management procedures is not in its best interest. According to Ted Thompson, executive vice president of the International Council of Cruise Lines (ICCL), "As a business that is dependent on carrying passengers to beautiful locations where our passengers can experience nature's bounty, our membership recognizes that even a perception that the industry in not meeting U.S. or international standards is damaging to our image and therefore our business prospects." With this in mind, Thomson asserts, "the cruise industry has proactively established guidelines regarding environmental practices . . . that each of the lines has agreed it will adhere to."

Ocean and coastal conservation activists question this claim. These commentators argue that voluntary efforts have been inadequate to prevent cruise ship pollution. According to Kira Schmidt, director of Bluewater Network's Cruise Ship Campaign, which is working to strengthen laws regulating the cruise ship industry, "The cruise industry has a history of illegally polluting the waters in which it sails. From 1993 to 1998, cruise ships were held responsible for 104 confirmed cases of illegal discharge of oil, garbage, and hazardous wastes, and required to pay more than $30 million in fines." In one particularly egregious case, Royal Caribbean Cruises, Ltd. admitted it had routinely dumped waste oil, and hazardous photo processing, dry cleaning, and print-shop chemicals into U.S. harbors and coastal areas. Some investigators characterized the violations as a "fleet-wide conspiracy [to] use our nation's waterways as its dumping ground," Schmidt claims. The company admitted its guilt and agreed to pay a record $18 million in criminal fines.

Critics claim that the ease with which the cruise ship industry flouts existing pollution laws demonstrates the importance of enacting specialized federal laws to keep the industry in check. They argue that current laws regulating ships in U.S. waters are inadequate to protect against the dangerous quantity of waste these modern behemoths produce. "The Clean Water Act was formulated before the dawn of the mega-cruise ship, when waste from vessels was not perceived as a significant problem," Schmidt maintains. To tie up this loophole, the Ocean Conservancy contends, "Congress should pass national legislation banning the discharge of untreated sewage from cruise ships in all U.S. waters."

Whether new federal law should be passed to regulate cruise ship waste is one of several controversies in the debate over how the government can best reduce pollution. The authors in the following chapter discuss other controversies regarding the government's role in ensuring a clean environment.

| *"Clean Skies legislation . . . sets tough new*
standards to dramatically reduce the three
most significant forms of pollution."

Market-Based Air Pollution Laws Will Reduce Air Pollution

George W. Bush

The United States needs air pollution laws that promote economic growth, claims President George W. Bush in the following viewpoint. Traditional air pollution laws that require utilities to use costly pollution-reduction strategies inhibit economic growth, he contends, which then cuts resources needed to protect the environment. Congress should therefore support revised federal air pollution laws that not only cap the amount of air pollutants that utilities may produce but also reward utilities for using innovative, cost-effective pollution-reduction strategies, Bush maintains. This market-based approach, he argues, will protect Americans from dangerous pollutants and promote the U.S. economy.

As you read, consider the following questions:
1. According to Bush, what are the three most significant forms of pollution from power plants?
2. In the author's view, what program has cut more pollution in the last decade than all other programs under the 1990 Clean Air Act?
3. What would the approach taken under the Kyoto protocol have cost the American economy, in the author's opinion?

George W. Bush, speech before the National Oceanic and Atmospheric Administration, Silver Spring, Maryland, February 14, 2002.

It's an honor to join you all today to talk about our environment and about the prospect of dramatic progress to improve it.

Today, I'm announcing a new environmental approach that will clean our skies, bring greater health to our citizens and encourage environmentally responsible development in America and around the world.

Particularly, it's an honor to address this topic at NOAA [National Oceanic and Atmospheric Administration], whose research is providing us with the answers to critical questions about our environment. . . .

A Common Goal

America and the world share this common goal: we must foster economic growth in ways that protect our environment. We must encourage growth that will provide a better life for citizens, while protecting the land, the water, and the air that sustain life.

In pursuit of this goal, my government has set two priorities: we must clean our air, and we must address the issue of global climate change. We must also act in a serious and responsible way, given the scientific uncertainties. While these uncertainties remain, we can begin now to address the human factors that contribute to climate change. Wise action now is an insurance policy against future risks.

I have been working with my Cabinet to meet these challenges with forward and creative thinking. I said, if need be, let's challenge the status quo. But let's always remember, let's do what is in the interest of the American people.

Today, I'm confident that the environmental path that I announce will benefit the entire world. This new approach is based on this common-sense idea: that economic growth is key to environmental progress, because it is growth that provides the resources for investment in clean technologies.

This new approach will harness the power of markets, the creativity of entrepreneurs, and draw upon the best scientific research. And it will make possible a new partnership with the developing world to meet our common environmental and economic goals.

We will apply this approach first to the challenge of cleaning the air that Americans breathe. Today, I call for new Clean Skies legislation[1] that sets tough new standards to dramatically reduce the three most significant forms of pollution from power plants, sulfur dioxide, nitrogen oxides and mercury.

We will cut sulfur dioxide emissions by 73 percent from current levels. We will cut nitrogen oxide emissions by 67 percent. And, for the first time ever, we will cap emissions of mercury, cutting them by 69 percent. These cuts will be completed over two measured phases, with one set of emission limits for 2010 and for the other for 2018.

This legislation will constitute the most significant step America has ever taken—has ever taken—to cut power plant emissions that contribute to urban smog, acid rain and numerous health problems for our citizens.

Clean Skies legislation will not only protect our environment, it will prolong the lives of thousands of Americans with asthma and other respiratory illnesses, as well as with those with heart disease. And it will reduce the risk to children exposed to mercury during a mother's pregnancy.

Harnessing the Power of Markets

The Clean Skies legislation will reach our ambitious air quality goals through a market-based cap-and-trade approach that rewards innovation, reduces cost and guarantees results. Instead of the government telling utilities where and how to cut pollution, we will tell them when and how much to cut. We will give them a firm deadline and let them find the most innovative ways to meet it.

We will do this by requiring each facility to have a permit for each ton of pollution it emits. By making the permits tradeable, this system makes it financially worthwhile for companies to pollute less, giving them an incentive to make early and cost effective reductions.

This approach enjoys widespread support, with both Democrats and Republicans, because we know it works. You see, since 1995 we have used a cap-and-trade program for sulfur dioxide pollution. It has cut more air pollution, this

---

1. As of January 2005, both S. 485 and H.R. 999, bills to amend the Clean Air Act, remain in committee.

system has reduced more air pollution in the last decade than all other programs under the 1990 Clean Air Act combined. And by even more than the law required. Compliance has been virtually 100 percent. It takes only a handful of employees to administer this program. And no one had to enter a courtroom to make sure the reductions happened.

Because the system gives businesses an incentive to create and install innovative technologies, these reductions have cost about 80 percent less than expected. It helps to keep energy prices affordable for our consumers. And we made this progress during a decade when our economy, and our demand for energy, was growing.

The Clean Skies legislation I propose is structured on this approach because it works. It will replace a confusing, ineffective maze of regulations for power plants that has created an endless cycle of litigation. Today, hundreds of millions of dollars are spent on lawyers, rather than on environmental protection. The result is painfully slow, uncertain and expensive programs on clean air.

Instead, Clean Skies legislation will put less money into paying lawyers and regulators, and money directly into programs to reduce pollution, to meet our national goal. This approach, I'm absolutely confident, will bring better and faster results in cleaning up our air.

Stabilizing Greenhouse Gases

Now, global climate change presents a different set of challenges and requires a different strategy. The science is more complex, the answers are less certain, and the technology is less developed. So we need a flexible approach that can adjust to new information and new technology.

I reaffirm America's commitment to the United Nations Framework Convention and its central goal, to stabilize atmospheric greenhouse gas concentrations at a level that will prevent dangerous human interference with the climate. Our immediate goal is to reduce America's greenhouse gas emissions relative to the size of our economy.

My administration is committed to cutting our nation's greenhouse gas intensity—how much we emit per unit of economic activity—by 18 percent over the next 10 years.

This will set America on a path to slow the growth of our greenhouse gas emissions and, as science justifies, to stop and then reverse the growth of emissions.

This is the common sense way to measure progress. Our nation must have economic growth—growth to create opportunity; growth to create a higher quality of life for our citizens. Growth is also what pays for investments in clean technologies, increased conservation, and energy efficiency. Meeting our commitment to reduce our greenhouse gas intensity by 18 percent by the year 2012 will prevent over 500 million metric tons of greenhouse gases from going into the atmosphere over the course of the decade. And that is the equivalent of taking 70 million cars off the road.

To achieve this goal, our nation must move forward on many fronts, looking at every sector of our economy. We will challenge American businesses to further reduce emissions. Already, agreements with the semiconductor and aluminum industries and others have dramatically cut emissions of some of the most potent greenhouse gases. We will build on these successes with new agreements and greater reductions.

Our government will also move forward immediately to create world-class standards for measuring and registering emission reductions. And we will give transferable credits to companies that can show real emission reductions.

We will promote renewable energy production and clean coal technology, as well as nuclear power, which produces no greenhouse gas emissions. And we will work to safely improve fuel economy for our cars and our trucks.

Using Sound Science

Overall, my budget devotes $4.5 billion to addressing climate change—more than any other nation's commitment in the entire world. This is an increase of more than $700 million over last year's budget. Our nation will continue to lead the world in basic climate and science research to address gaps in our knowledge that are important to decision makers.

When we make decisions, we want to make sure we do so on sound science; not what sounds good, but what is real. And the United States leads the world in providing that kind of research. We'll devote $588 million towards the research and development of energy conservation technologies. We must and we will conserve more in the United States. And we will spend $408 million toward research and development on renewables, on renewable energy.

This funding includes $150 million for an initiative that [Energy Secretary] Spence Abraham laid out the other day, $150 million for the Freedom Car Initiative, which will advance the prospect of breakthrough zero-emission fuel cell technologies.

Clear Skies Emissions Caps

	Actual Emissions in 2000	First Phase of Reductions	Second Phase of Reductions	Total Reduction
Sulfur Dioxide	11.2 million tons	4.5 million tons in 2010	3 million tons in 2018	73%
Nitrogen Oxides	5.1 million tons	2.1 million tons in 2008	1.7 million tons in 2018	67%
Mercury	48 tons	26 tons in 2010	15 tons in 2018	69%

Environmental Protection Agency, "Clear Skies Act of 2003," February 2003.

My comprehensive energy plan, the first energy plan that any administration has put out in a long period of time, provides $4.6 billion over the next five years in clean energy tax incentives to encourage purchases of hybrid and fuel cell vehicles, to promote residential solar energy, and to reward investments in wind, solar and biomass energy production. And we will look for ways to increase the amount of carbon stored by America's farms and forests through a strong conservation title in the farm bill. I have asked [Agriculture] Secretary [Ann M.] Veneman to recommend new targeted incentives for landowners to increase carbon storage.

By doing all these things, by giving companies incentives to cut emissions, by diversifying our energy supply to include cleaner fuels, by increasing conservation, by increasing research and development and tax incentives for energy efficiency and clean technologies, and by increasing carbon storage, I am absolutely confident that America will reach the goal that I have set.

If, however, by 2012, our progress is not sufficient and sound science justifies further action, the United States will respond with additional measures that may include broad-based market programs as well as additional incentives and voluntary measures designed to accelerate technology development and deployment.

Addressing global climate change will require a sustained effort over many generations. My approach recognizes that economic growth is the solution, not the problem. Because a nation that grows its economy is a nation that can afford investments and new technologies.

An Unsound Treaty

The approach taken under the Kyoto protocol would have required the United States to make deep and immediate cuts in our economy to meet an arbitrary target. It would have cost our economy up to $400 billion and we would have lost 4.9 million jobs.

As President of the United States, charged with safeguarding the welfare of the American people and American workers, I will not commit our nation to an unsound international treaty that will throw millions of our citizens out of work. Yet, we recognize our international responsibilities. So in addition to acting here at home, the United States will actively help developing nations grow along a more efficient, more environmentally responsible path.

The hope of growth and opportunity and prosperity is universal. It's the dream and right of every society on our globe. The United States wants to foster economic growth in the developing world, including the world's poorest nations. We want to help them realize their potential, and bring the benefits of growth to their peoples, including better health, and better schools and a cleaner environment.

It would be unfair—indeed, counterproductive—to condemn developing nations to slow growth or no growth by insisting that they take on impractical and unrealistic greenhouse gas targets. Yet, developing nations such as China and India already account for a majority of the world's greenhouse gas emissions, and it would be irresponsible to absolve them from shouldering some of the shared obligations.

The greenhouse gas intensity approach I put forward to-day gives developing countries a yardstick for progress on climate change that recognizes their right to economic development. I look forward to discussing this new approach next week [in February 2003], when I go to China and Japan and South Korea. The United States will not interfere with the plans of any nation that chooses to ratify the Kyoto protocol. But I will intend to work with nations, especially the poor and developing nations, to show the world that there is a better approach, that we can build our future prosperity along a cleaner and better path.

Sharing U.S. Technology

My budget includes over $220 million for the U.S. Agency for International Development and a global environmental facility to help developing countries better measure, reduce emissions, and to help them invest in clean and renewable energy technologies. Many of these technologies, which we take for granted in our own country, are not being used in the developing world. We can help ensure that the benefits of these technologies are more broadly shared. Such efforts have helped bring solar energy to Bangladesh, hydroelectric energy to the Philippines, geothermal electricity to Kenya. These projects are bringing jobs and environmental benefits to these nations, and we will build on these successes.

The new budget also provides $40 million under the Tropical Forest Conservation Act to help countries redirect debt payments towards protecting tropical forests, forests that store millions of tons of carbon. And I've also ordered the Secretary of State to develop a new initiative to help developing countries stop illegal logging, a practice that destroys biodiversity and releases millions of tons of greenhouse gases into the atmosphere.

And, finally, my government is following through on our commitment to provide $25 million for climate observation systems in developing countries that will help scientists understand the dynamics of climate change.

To clean the air, and to address climate change, we need to recognize that economic growth and environmental protection go hand in hand. Affluent societies are the ones that demand, and can therefore afford, the most environmental protection. Prosperity is what allows us to commit more and more resources to environmental protection. And in the coming decades, the world needs to develop and deploy billions of dollars of technologies that generate energy in cleaner ways. And we need strong economic growth to make that possible.

Americans are among the most creative people in our history. We have used radio waves to peer into the deepest reaches of space. We cracked life's genetic code. We have made our air and land and water significantly cleaner, even as we have built the world's strongest economy.

When I see what Americans have done, I know what we can do. We can tap the power of economic growth to further protect our environment for generations that follow. And that's what we're going to do.

"We are likely to see even fewer [emission] reductions because the proposed rule is less stringent than the original Clear Skies legislation."

Market-Based Air Pollution Laws Will Increase Air Pollution

Eric Schaeffer

Relaxing laws that regulate power plant emissions will increase air pollution, argues Eric Schaeffer in the following viewpoint. New legislation proposed by the Bush administration has been drafted under the influence of the utilities it will regulate and will therefore benefit them at the expense of Americans' health, he claims. According to Schaeffer, evidence refutes the administration's claim that market-based strategies are more likely to reduce pollution than Clean Air Act rules already in place. Market-based approaches such as the cap and trade program, whereby industries can buy the right to increase their emissions by purchasing emission credits from industries that are below emission caps, will result in more pollution, he maintains. Schaeffer, director of the Environmental Integrity Project, was director of the Environmental Protection Agency from 2001 until 2002.

As you read, consider the following questions:
1. What is the most outrageous example of how the energy industry has influenced the Environmental Protection Agency, in Schaeffer's view?
2. According to the author, why will those companies that violate the weaker New Source Review regulations be much harder to catch?

Eric Schaeffer, testimony before the U.S. Senate Democratic Policy Committee, Washington, DC, February 6, 2004.

M y name is Eric Schaeffer and I was Director of the Environmental Protection Agency's Office of Regulatory Enforcement before resigning two years ago [in 2002].

A Legacy of Pollution

I have been invited to talk about the legacy of pollution from a fleet of electric power plants built in the nineteen fifties and sixties that do not yet meet the air pollution control requirements established in the nineteen seventies. These power plants, owned by just a handful of very big companies, are responsible for two-thirds of the sulfur dioxide and one quarter of the nitrogen oxides emitted from all sources in the U.S. today. Scientists over the past decade have determined that these pollutants combine with ammonia in the atmosphere to form fine particle pollution that robs our lungs of their ability to absorb oxygen, which in turn triggers asthma attacks, chronic bronchitis, and lung and heart disease. From EPA estimates, we know that fine particle pollution from power plants contributes to more than 20,000 premature deaths every year.

If these grim statistics are not enough, the same plants are responsible for one-third of the airborne mercury emissions released every year from all sources. These emissions damage waterways and contaminate humans exposed to the high levels of mercury that bioaccumulate in fish. Because mercury is a potent neurotoxin, especially dangerous to infants in the earliest stage of development, it is particularly alarming to hear from the Centers for Disease Control that one out of twelve women of childbearing age have unsafe levels of mercury in their blood.

These estimates of risk, which the Bush Administration accepts, suggest that we have a public health crisis that demands an urgent response from government, not politics as usual. What has the Administration done?

- It has crippled enforcement of the very laws that require cleanup of these power plants;
- It has invited the same companies that the Justice Department has accused of violating the Clean Air Act to rewrite the law in their favor;
- It has promoted relaxed, polluter friendly approaches that would delay cleanup for decades.

Environmental Enforcement Undermined

[In the late 1990s,] the Justice Department filed lawsuits against some of the biggest power companies in America, alleging that they had modified their boilers and illegally increased emissions without obtaining permits and upgrading pollution controls as required by the Clean Air Act's "New Source Review" [NSR] provisions. From its first day in office [in 2001] the Bush Administration set about undermining these enforcement actions through rule changes that inflated exemptions to the point where New Source Review is now more loophole than law. One rule change allows a company to replace up to twenty percent of an entire plant, increasing pollution by thousands of tons in the process, while pretending that these investments are no more than routine repair activities that are exempt from the law.

The Administration has stubbornly insisted that pollution will not increase under this new loophole. [In August 2003,] a federal court in Ohio found that First Energy Corporation had undertaken eleven unpermitted modifications at its Sammis [Ohio] plant, which resulted in thousands of tons of illegal increases of sulfur dioxide and nitrogen oxide. All of these projects would be exempt today, because they cost far less than the new twenty percent threshold for exemption in the Administration's new rule. I wrote to the Agency [in November 2003] asking them if in fact the First Energy projects the court found had illegally increased pollution would be exempt under the new rule, but have yet to receive a reply.

While the Justice Department has continued work on the handful of court cases it inherited from the previous Administration, until [January 2004] it had filed no new complaints against approximately seventy companies under investigation for New Source Review violations, even though some of those had been referred to the Justice Department for prosecution years ago. In fact, in November [2003] the EPA's Assistant Administrator for Enforcement specifically directed the regions to drop those investigations, at the direction of either the White House or someone else inside the EPA. In December [2003], the DC Circuit [Court] stayed the Bush Administration's most significant rollback of NSR regulations, so [in January 2004] the Justice Department dusted off and finally filed a complaint against the Eastern Kentucky power plant. But the Justice Department's position has already been compromised by having to justify to courts its attempt to enforce a law that its clients at EPA are desperately trying to repeal. . . .

There is no happy ending to the trap the Bush Administration has set for its own attorneys. At best, power companies have been able to delay for another three years a final reckoning with pollution control standards that have been in place for nearly thirty years. But the crippling of enforcement cases offers only the most outrageous example of how completely the energy industry has captured the Agency that is supposed to be its regulator.

The Energy Lobby Takes Over EPA

We learned in the *Washington Post* that some sections of the preamble to EPA's new mercury rule were lifted verbatim from a submittal by Latham and Watkins, [corporate] lawyers representing power companies. Last fall [2003], a U.S. General Accounting Office report suggested that decisions to weaken New Source Review rules were driven by unexamined anecdotes from the very industries that benefited from the rule changes. The week after EPA announced the virtual repeal of New Source Review regulations, the chief of staff of the Office of Air and Radiation went to work for the Southern Company, one of the nation's largest electric utilities and a principal defendant in the Clean Air Act lawsuits. EPA's former head of Congressional Affairs has taken up his new assignment with the National Electricity Reliability Coordinating Council, the lobbying outfit formed to fight EPA's enforcement actions.

The cartel of lawyers and lobbyists that run EPA's Office of Air and Radiation are making sure that any laws that do survive will be much harder to enforce. Those few companies that somehow find a way to violate the much weaker New Source Review regulations will be much harder to catch, according to the GAO [General Accounting Office], because key reporting requirements were eliminated. And [in January 2004], EPA decided to surrender its authority to require tougher emissions monitoring in air permits to "settle" a lawsuit brought by its industry friends, even though a virtually identical suit had been thrown out of court. The Administration's campaign fundraising network of "pioneers" and "rangers" includes companies, lawyers and lobbyists fighting to hamstring enforcement of the Clean Air Act.

Selling the Rollbacks

While campaign contributions play a role, I don't doubt that Bush Administration policies are also fueled by a deep ideological hostility to the laws enacted by Congress to safeguard our environment and protect public health. These ideological blinders may explain why the Administration so often appears to operate in a "fact free" zone when promoting its alternatives. The EPA has made no secret of its desire to eliminate permits that require each plant to use the best available technology to reduce emissions, in favor of allowing the market trading of pollution rights under a national emissions ceiling. That has led the Administration to propose allowing utilities to buy and sell the right to emit mercury, a deadly neurotoxin, as though it were pork bellies or some other innocuous commodity.[1]

The Administration brushes off critics by saying that its mercury trading program will reduce emissions much further and faster than traditional alternatives. How much faster? Governor Leavitt told power company executives gathered at the Edison Electric Institute on January 9 [2004] that EPA's proposal would cut mercury emissions seventy percent over the next fifteen years, from 48 tons today to 15 tons by 2018. That 70 percent reduction is also reflected in EPA fact sheets and the preamble of the proposed rule. But EPA's own data show that we'll be lucky to get a 50% reduction in mercury over the next twenty years under the Agency's "cap and trade" proposal.

The Integrated Planning Model that EPA uses to project power plant emissions, which was updated in 2003 and is available on the Agency's website, projects that mercury emissions under Clear Skies would reduce emissions from

1. As of January 2005, both S. 485 and H.R. 999, bills to amend the Clean Air Act, to allow such trading, remain in committee.

today's 48 tons to 22.2 tons somewhere between 2018 and 2022. That represents a 54% reduction, not the 70% promised in EPA's public statements. But we are likely to see even fewer reductions because the proposed rule is less stringent than the original Clear Skies legislation, in allowing greater emissions of mercury in the near-term.

"Clear Skies" Means More Soot and Smog		
	Sulfur Dioxide (SO_2)	Nitrogen Oxides (NO_2)
EPA Proposal (Aug 2001)	2 million tons in 2010	1.9 million tons in 2008 1.25 million tons in 2012
Administration Plan	4.5 million tons in 2010 3 million tons in 2018	2.1 million tons in 2008 1.7 million tons in 2018

Clear the Air, "Doing the Math," www.cleartheair.org, n.d.

This slower rate of reductions is in part a consequence of the "emissions banking" established under the trading program. Under EPA's proposal, each company receives a set number of pollution allowances (i.e., the right to emit a certain amount of mercury), but can emit pollution above that amount by either buying allowances from other companies or accumulating unused allowances from earlier years.

In the first years of the program, EPA expects to distribute more mercury pollution allowances than industry actually needs. These "surplus" allowances can be stored away and used in later years, when lower emission ceilings shrink the supply of new emission credits. The Administration also shuts off the requirement to reduce mercury emissions when control costs get too "expensive," although it has not explained why such controls are not affordable.

How Long Can We Afford to Wait?

Many of EPA's adventures in rewriting the Clean Air Act seem destined for a bad end. The DC Circuit [Court] has already stayed the most important New Source Review rollback, which seems likely to be struck down once the court hears arguments on the merits. States and environmental groups will challenge the mercury rule and the rollbacks in air emission monitoring, and seem equally likely to prevail. The Bush Administration likes to boast about how it is getting rid of lawyers, but its wild and fact-free forays into rule-making will force us all to slog through the courts for years to come. These delays benefit no one but the handful of big power companies still fighting a Clean Air Act passed by Congress [in 1970].

But now, our scientists have put us on notice that further delays will come at a terrible cost to the public health. In the two hours it will take to hold this hearing, another five lives will be cut short from fine particle pollution from power plants, and more than thirty infants will face mercury exposures that increase the risk of developmental disorders. How much longer can we afford to wait?

> "*[Twenty nine toxic waste] cleanup projects in 17 states . . . stalled out because they were underfunded.*"

Funding for the Superfund Toxic Waste Cleanup Program Should Be Increased

Amanda Griscom

The Superfund, a federal toxic-waste cleanup program, should receive increased funding, argues Amanda Griscom in the following viewpoint. Toxic waste continues to be a serious problem in America, yet the Superfund budget has dwindled. In consequence, the number of sites cleaned up each year has dropped substantially since the program was established in 1980, she claims. Griscom writes for *Grist* magazine, an environmental news magazine.

As you read, consider the following questions:

1. In Griscom's view, how did the number of toxic waste sites cleaned up in 2003 differ from the number cleaned up per year between 1996 and 2000?
2. In the author's opinion, if the polluter tax is no longer collected, who will be stuck with the bill for the clean up of orphan sites?
3. According to the author, how many Americans live within four miles of a Superfund site?

A rsenic in water, mercury emissions, new-source review,[1] [Vice President] Dick Cheney's energy task force—these are the issues that have elicited the loudest howls of protest about the Bush administration's environmental record. . . . By comparison, the grumbling over Superfund[2] has been remarkably muted.

But lately the grumble has risen to a growl. In mid-April [2004], *Time* ran a feature by Margot Roosevelt entitled "The Tragedy of Tar Creek," which exposed what it called "eco-assault on an epic scale." The article looked at a neglected Superfund site that has led to widespread lead poisoning, among other scourges, in a nearby Oklahoma community—where "Little League fields have been built over an immense underground cavity that could collapse at any time. Acid mine waste flushes into drinking wells . . . [and] neon-orange scum oozes onto the roadside. Wild onions, a regional delicacy tossed into scrambled eggs, are saturated with cadmium."

Underfunded Cleanup Projects

It's one thing to lament this particularly egregious case; it's another to accept that the Tar Creek tragedy is just one of many Superfund screw-ups. As Roosevelt's article pointed out, Tar Creek can be counted among 29 other cleanup projects in 17 states that stalled out because they were underfunded by the U.S. EPA [Environmental Protection Agency] [in 2003], according to the agency's inspector general's office.

Since President [George W.] Bush took office, the Superfund program's budget has decreased by 25 percent in inflation-adjusted dollars, and some 50 percent fewer sites have been cleaned up, according to a report produced by the Sierra Club [a U.S. environmental organization] and the U.S. Public Interest Research Group [PIRG] Education Fund. In fiscal year 2003, the Bush administration completed cleanups at only 40 Superfund toxic-waste sites,

---

1. This refers to a Clean Air Act requirement that requires a review of any new facility that has the potential to emit air pollutants in amounts specified by law. The review establishes the impact of the pollution and the options available to control that pollution.   2. Superfund is a federal program to locate, investigate, and clean up the worst uncontrolled and abandoned toxic waste sites nationwide. The fund is administered by the Environmental Protection Agency.

whereas an average of 87 Superfund cleanups were completed per year between 1996 and 2000.

Industry representatives and Bush officials argue that these numbers are misleading because many of the easiest-to-tackle Superfund sites were cleaned up early in the program's history, leaving behind bigger, more complex sites that take longer to deal with. Environmentalists counter that so-called "mega-sites" have been part of the agency's agenda for decades, and the shortfall is due to meager funding and a flimsy commitment to the Superfund cause.

"The Bush administration has watched the Superfund program dwindle to a shadow of itself. It's in the worst shape since it was passed by Congress in 1980," said Grant Cope, an environmental attorney who specializes in toxic waste. "The data unequivocally show that there has been a dramatic slowdown in the pace of cleanups at the nation's worst toxic-waste sites and a reduction in the number of new sites that EPA is listing as eligible for cleanup. Both problems are due to gross deficiencies in funding."

Granted, this is partly attributable to circumstances that pre-date the Bush administration. In 1995, the GOP [Republican] majority in Congress refused to reauthorize a tax levied on polluting industries that supplied the grubstake for the Superfund and enabled the EPA to clean up contaminated sites even if the costs were too high for a polluting company to handle. That tax hasn't been renewed since.

Then again, the Bush administration is the first ever to argue against the tax and refuse to advocate for it on the Hill; moreover, the administration has made only meager efforts to replenish the fund by other means. Although the White House did request an increase in Superfund allocations for fiscal year 2004, which Congress refused to grant, "it was clear their request was placed at the bottom of their list of priorities," said Cope. "Over and over again, this is an administration that has proven it can force its priorities through Congress. Superfund is simply not a priority."

A Questionable Report

But while the Bush administration has been remiss on the funding front, it did make an effort to shape the future of

Superfund through creating a subcommittee under the EPA's National Advisory Council for Environmental Policy and Technology (NACEPT). After 22 months of investigation and debate, and more than 1 million in taxpayer dollars to fund the deliberations, the subcommittee released its report in mid-April [2004] with recommendations for the Superfund program. That report got virtually no media coverage, other than a brief mention in the *Time* article as the reason that Superfund advocates are "bracing for a new battle."

"While the [subcommittee] process highlighted the need to address serious problems with the Bush administration's implementation of the program, the report was biased, unacceptable, and off the mark," said Cope, one of the subcommittee's 32 members. So unacceptable did he find its recommendations, in fact, that he was one of five subcommittee members who refused to sign the final document. Other dissenters included representatives from the Sierra Club, the Center for Public Environmental Oversight, the New Jersey Department of Environmental Protection, and the Mineral Policy Center (now known as Earthworks).

Chief among their concerns was that the report's conclusions disproportionately represented the interests of an industry-stacked panel: "Two-thirds of committee members represented the interests of PRPs [potentially responsible parties]—corporations responsible for toxic-waste sites listed on [Superfund's] National Priorities List," said Vicky Peters, a subcommittee participant from the Colorado attorney general's office. "Not just executives, but people who have a stake in the PRPs—scrap recyclers, lobbyists, insurers, legal reps, developers. These are all people who have liabilities or who represent companies with liabilities."

Not surprisingly, the industry-heavy committee blocked any recommendations that would increase funding for the Superfund program—presumably for fear that it would empower the EPA to issue more administrative orders forcing them to pony up cleanup funds. . . .

Who Should Pay?

While . . . roughly 70 percent of all Superfund cleanups are paid for directly by the polluters, some 30 percent are so-called orphan sites that have either been abandoned or that polluters don't have the funds to deal with. That's where the polluter tax comes in: The pooled tax revenues from chemical-producing and polluting industries pay for orphan-site cleanups as well as for oversight on the other projects. But with the tax no longer being collected, mom-and-pop taxpayers are stuck with the bill. In 2004, taxpayers [were] expected to pay more than $1 billion for Superfund cleanups—roughly 300 percent more than they paid for the program in 1995, according to a U.S. PIRG analysis.

Cleaning Up the Mess

Cleaning up chemical waste is a public health necessity. . . . Any kindergardener will tell you that if you make a mess, you have to clean it up. Shifting the cost burden from the polluting industries responsible for creating the toxic waste to the taxpayers is neither fair nor sound public policy.

Bob Smith, "Superfund Tax Commentary," www.senatorbobsmith.org, October 20, 2003.

Industry argues that the polluter tax is unfair because "it flies in the face of individual accountability. It's just generic accountability," says Briggum. "Should a company help pay for a contaminated site even if they didn't contaminate it, just because they are part of an industry—or should general revenues be used? I don't think it's self-evident who it ought to be."

To environmentalists (and even to the Reagan and Bush I administrations, which supported the polluter tax), the logic was clear enough. As Cope explains it, "If industries are earning profits off the sale and use of products that contaminate the environment, they are more directly associated with [the consequences] than taxpayers."

In March [2004], Senate Democrats lost an effort to reinstate the polluter tax by only seven votes. That prompted the Sierra Club to air TV spots in swing states with a "Make Polluters Pay" slogan, and on tax day, enviros protested at post offices in 25 states to drive the issue home to taxpayers.

Still, industry-oriented members of the subcommittee managed to keep a funding recommendation out of the NACEPT report entirely, arguing that money is Congress' domain and the subcommittee should focus on the way Superfund is managed, a matter that the EPA can directly control.

A Need for Funding

Environmentalists decried this effort to pass the buck: "Well, if the EPA isn't going to ask Congress for money, who the heck will?" asked Cope. . . .

Midway through the subcommittee deliberations, when it became apparent that members would never reach consensus on most major issues, EPA gave up on that approach and advised the members to submit a range of views. Problem is, the range of views were mostly published without attribution, and many that came from industry could weaken Superfund's protections. "The final conclusions drawn in the report totally lacked accountability, and basically gave [industry's unattributed recommendations] as much legitimacy and weight as the consensus recommendations," said Jessica Frohman, a Sierra Club toxic-waste specialist who served as an alternate representative on the subcommittee.

Every dissenter who refused to sign the report agreed that its first major flaw was the failure to acknowledge the need for a significant, stable funding source and to even entertain the idea of reinstituting the tax on polluting industries. The program's dire funding shortages were even acknowledged in an internal EPA report quietly posted on the agency's website, although no real funding solutions were proposed. Among the range of recommendations that dissenting subcommittee members found problematic was the notion that sites be added to Superfund's National Priority List based on EPA's budgetary constraints, weighing the financial viability of site cleanups instead of focusing on how much of a threat sites pose to public health. Even more alarming to some was the suggestion that sites be cleaned up based on their potential to be redeveloped for commercial purposes—a proposal that would disadvantage the cleanup of sites in rural communities and inner-city areas, which are generally less favorable markets for commercial development.

"The most discouraging thing that came out of this committee meeting is that it could change the fundamental mission of Superfund," said Frohman. "This was a program developed first and foremost to protect human health, to save lives. These recommendations have the potential to turn it into a program contingent on expenses and affordability, rather than protecting public health."

Cope also has concerns about the report's potential ramifications: "If the Bush administration gets reelected, I think that . . . officials could use [the report] to weaken the program—either to change the statutory language or undertake more subtle administrative reforms. And the report would give them political cover to do so."[3]

These concerns loom large when you consider that one out of every four Americans lives within four miles of a Superfund site, according to the General Accounting Office. That translates into 73 million Americans who could be at risk of floating down Love Canal[4] if Superfund continues to be neglected.

3. Bush was reelected in November 2004.   4. Love Canal, located near Niagara Falls, New York, is a housing development built near a toxic waste dump containing thousands of steel drums of chemical waste. Some twenty-five years after they had been dumped at this site, the drums had corroded, and toxic gases were rising to the surface, posing a threat to area residents. The name has for many become synonymous with the toxic waste problem.

VIEWPOINT 4

> "*Congress should incinerate [the Superfund toxic waste cleanup program], dump its ashes in a landfill with an impermeable liner, and pave over the landfill to ensure the program never comes back.*"

The Superfund Toxic Waste Cleanup Program Should Be Abolished

Steven Milloy

Congress should abolish the federal toxic-waste cleanup program known as Superfund, argues Steven Milloy in the following viewpoint. There is no evidence that contaminants at Superfund sites threaten public health, he claims, yet thousands of lives are lost while cleaning up Superfund sites. Moreover, Milloy maintains, forcing businesses to pay the cost of cleaning up sites when they are not responsible for the waste dumped there is unfair. Milloy is an adjunct scholar with the Cato Institute, a libertarian think tank, and author of *Junk Science Judo: Self-Defense Against Health Scares and Scams*.

As you read, consider the following questions:
1. According to Milloy, how were sites selected to be on the National Priorities List?
2. In the author's view, what is the actual casualty toll at Superfund sites?
3. When did Congress let the tax that funded the Superfund program expire?

"Almost one in 10 of the nation's 1,230 Superfund toxic waste sites have not yet been cleaned up enough to guarantee that people and drinking water supplies won't become contaminated," reported the Associated Press.

"Environmentalists said those figures show the Bush administration is failing to protect public health, and Congress and the White House should reinstate a special tax to help fund the Superfund program," the AP continued.

But this . . . attack on President [George W.] Bush by environmental extremists rings hollow, which becomes clear once the Superfund program's dirty secrets are revealed.

Revealing Dirty Secrets

Superfund is the federal program providing for the clean-up of so-called toxic waste sites. The law was hastily passed after the 1980 elections by a lame-duck Congress and signed into law by a lame-duck President [Jimmy] Carter.

And all that lame-ness became part-and-parcel of the Superfund program.

Clean-ups of Superfund sites were begun regardless of actual risks to local residents and environment, and regardless of cost. The Environmental Protection Agency [EPA] infamously compelled site clean-ups based on unrealistic future scenarios such as a child consuming a teaspoon of the most contaminated soil from the middle of a landfill every day for years.

Sites originally selected to be cleaned up, the so-called National Priorities List, were not selected on the basis of threat to the local community or environment but on spreading the wealth. The National Priorities List was established so that every state could have a Superfund site, no doubt because the clean-up program was more about local jobs than environmental protection.

Businesses and landowners were forced to pay for clean-ups regardless whether they were responsible for disposing wastes at the sites and even if the disposals were done according to the existing law at the time.

Superfund clean-up became a booming industry with about $50 billion in revenues by the mid-1990s. The Government Accounting Office projected in 2001 that as much as $300 billion will be required to clean up government-owned Superfund sites alone.

A Lack of Evidence

And so we come to the most important but least known of Superfund's "dirty" secrets—there has never been a single shred of evidence and not a single documented case of anyone ever becoming ill, getting cancer or dying because of contaminants at a Superfund site. That is based on my personal review of, and subsequent testimony to Congress in 1995 about, the records of more than 1,300 Superfund site histories prepared by the EPA. I have not seen any evidence or heard of any credible claim since that would change that.

A Costly Program

Even though Superfund appears to be like mom and apple pie, it is not. In reality, it gives the EPA [Environmental Protection Agency] billions of dollars to spend on an inefficient, costly, feel-good program that does little to reduce human health risks. Truly hazardous waste sites (if there are any) can be cleaned up without Superfund. The difference would be that the EPA would have to justify the worthiness of such projects against other projects considered for federal funding.

Peter VanDoren and Michael Gough, *Washington Times*, July 18, 2002.

Despite all the type and hysteria about the supposed dangers posed by dreaded "toxic" waste sites, the actual casualty toll at Superfund sites according to the EPA's records amounted to the following: some "number" of pine trees, a few thousand fish, fewer than 100 cattle, six birds and three ponies.

Even at the headline-grabbing Love Canal site[1] or the Woburn, Mass.,[2] site featured in the John Travolta movie "A Civil Action," multiple studies have subsequently been un-

---

1. Love Canal, located near Niagara Falls, New York, is a housing development built near a toxic waste dump containing thousands of steel drums of chemical waste. Some 25 years after they had been dumped at this site, the drums had corroded, and toxic gases were rising to the surface, posing a threat to area residents. The name has for many become synonymous with the toxic waste problem. 2. The Woburn toxic-waste lawsuit was a landmark federal case brought by eight families who accused W.R. Grace and Co. and other companies of contaminating their water, causing illness and death. Grace settled with the families. Exactly who was responsible for the contamination remains disputed.

able to link the sites with any actual health effects in local populations.

A Threat to Superfund Workers

Another dirty secret of the Superfund program is that, while there is no evidence anyone has been harmed by the contamination at Superfund sites, perhaps thousands of workers and others have been killed or injured as a result of construction and traffic accidents related to clean-ups.

According to a 1994 study by researchers at the National Safety Council, the likelihood of a fatality associated with excavation at a Superfund site is nearly 15 percent.

Workers have been killed removing and cleaning underground storage tanks. A man was killed and 87 others injured when a backhoe dislodged a gas pipeline and gas flowed into an adjacent senior citizens' home in Allentown, Pa., in 1994.

Hospital attention was required by 116 factory workers in 1986, when a truck containing hazardous waste mistakenly spilled its contents into the factory ventilation system.

There are also numerous examples of hazardous wastes being spilled during transport to landfills and incinerators.

None of this advocates nonremediation of sites contaminated with wastes or sites where wastes are improperly disposed. They should be cleaned up, but only to that extent that makes sense—something not possible under the current Superfund law.

Environmental extremists now want to reimpose a tax on businesses to pay for the Superfund program. Because the Superfund program and the EPA were messes themselves, Congress wisely let the tax expire in 1995 and has not come close to re-enacting it since.

Over the last 24 years, the Superfund program has killed and injured more people, wasted more money and accomplished less than any domestic federal environmental program.

Congress should incinerate Superfund, dump its ashes in a landfill with an impermeable liner, and pave over the landfill to ensure the program never comes back. Where toxic waste sites are a legitimate problem, we need a program that cost-effectively cleans up truly hazardous sites and that does not penalize (or kill) innocent parties.

"[Stricter rules] could have . . . some chance of actually succeeding in cleaning up the nation's worst polluted waters."

Federal Nonpoint Source Pollution Laws Should Be Strengthened

Richard A. Parrish

The Total Maximum Daily Load (TMDL) rule, which determines how much water pollution a source may discharge, is not reducing pollution because the government has not enforced it, claims Richard A. Parrish in the following viewpoint. Controlling nonpoint source pollution, pollution whose source cannot be determined, requires stricter TMDL rules, he argues. Requiring that states submit a detailed plan explaining how they will implement TMDL does not take authority away from the states, Parrish contends; it simply ensures that states present a viable strategy to reduce nonpoint source pollution. Parrish is an attorney with the Southern Environmental Law Center, an environmental advocacy organization.

As you read, consider the following questions:
1. In Parrish's opinion, what percentage of U.S. waters remains impaired?
2. In the author's view, why did the TMDL program lay dormant until the late 1980s?
3. According to the author, what is the most important lesson to be derived from the TMDL advisory committee?

Richard A. Parrish, testimony before the U.S. House Subcommittee on Water Resources and Environment, Committee on Transportation and Infrastructure, Washington, DC, February 15, 2000.

My name is Rick Parrish. I am an attorney with the Southern Environmental Law Center, a non-profit environmental advocacy group that works to protect public health and the environment in a six-state portion of the Southeast. I appreciate the opportunity to discuss with you today EPA's [Environmental Protection Agency's] . . . efforts to revitalize the Clean Water Act's watershed restoration or "Total Maximum Daily Load" (TMDL) program.[1]

EPA's proposed TMDL rules have come under attack from every conceivable direction. The intensity of this debate makes it easy to forget or overlook the following fundamental areas of general agreement.

Points of Agreement

Clean water and healthy aquatic ecosystems are of vital concern to the American public, now as in 1972 when the Clean Water Act was passed.

Almost 28 years after passage of the Clean Water Act, nearly 40 percent of the waters that are assessed nationwide remain impaired, that is, too polluted for fishing, swimming, and other designated or actual uses, including aquatic habitat.

States and EPA estimate that more than 20,000 water body segments are impaired, often by more than one pollutant, with the result that 40,000 TMDL-based clean-up plans will be required.

State monitoring programs cover only about one-third of our nation's waters. Even though new or better data will likely show that some currently listed waters do not, in fact, need TMDLs, the number of impaired waters nationwide is likely to increase as water quality monitoring programs expand in coverage.

The watershed approach to water quality planning and management is generally recognized as the most equitable and efficient method of protecting and restoring water quality, and the TMDL process is generally considered the technical backbone of that watershed approach.

---

1. The TMDL program, a part of the Clean Water Act, calculates the maximum amount of a pollutant that a water body can receive and still meet water quality standards, and allocates that amount to the pollutant's sources.

The TMDL program as currently designed is not succeeding in restoring water quality in impaired waters. We cannot afford to wait for perfect data and a perfect understanding of the interaction between pollutants and the aquatic ecosystem before taking steps to correct serious water pollution problems.

The states and EPA generally agree that non-point source activities are responsible for a majority of the impaired waters nationwide.

There is general agreement that additional funding will be required at the local, state, and federal level for the TMDL program to succeed nationwide. At the same time, there will likely be added costs if cleanups are delayed further, both in terms of the eventual expense of restoring water quality and the opportunity costs associated with reduced use, enjoyment and productivity of polluted waters.

Cleaning Up Impaired Waters

The overriding goal of the Federal Water Pollution Control Act, passed by Congress in 1972 and generally known as the Clean Water Act, was "to restore and maintain the chemical, physical, and biological integrity of the Nation's waters." While much progress has been made, especially with regard to the discharge of pollution from pipes and other point sources, the sad truth is that 40% of our nation's waters are still considered too polluted to be used for their intended purposes, including fishing, swimming, drinking, or as aquatic habitat. Section 303(d) of the Clean Water Act contains the one program specifically designed to deal with these impaired waters, the TMDL program. Section 303(d) requires states to identify their worst polluted waters and develop cleanup plans based on the calculation of the Total Maximum Daily Loads of particular pollutants that the water can accommodate. If states fail in these tasks, the duties revert to EPA. Designed to give states the primary role in cleaning up polluted waters, the TMDL program was largely ignored by states and EPA alike for over 20 years. In recent years, partly as a result of a wave of lawsuits filed by environmental groups, EPA has begun taking steps to implement the TMDL program to clean up the worst polluted waters in the country.

In my view, the single most significant step EPA has taken to revitalize the TMDL program is the proposal of rules that, for the most part, clarify and strengthen the requirements of the TMDL program. I believe that the heart of the proposed rules, the requirement that an implementation plan be developed as part of the TMDL itself, has the best chance of converting this watershed restoration initiative from a program marked by neglect and wasted effort to one marked by productivity and accomplishment over the years to come.

The Failure of the Original Program

The TMDL program lay dormant until the late 1980s when environmentalists starting filing citizen suits against EPA for allowing states to ignore their obligations to prepare lists of impaired waters and TMDL-based watershed recovery plans under Section 303(d). An Illinois case, *Scott v. City of Hammond*, established the principle that the state's failure to submit lists and TMDLs triggered EPA's mandatory duty to step into the void.

At this point, EPA has been sued in over half the states in the country for allowing the TMDL program to languish. In all but one such case (Minnesota), environmentalists have either won in court or negotiated a favorable settlement. At the same time the litigation was occurring, state and federal regulators were moving towards a watershed approach to water quality planning and management. EPA had issued TMDL regulations in 1985, modified them in 1992 to require state submittal of 303(d) lists every other year, and produced a series of programmatic guidance documents and policy statements throughout the 1990s to clarify how states should compile their 303(d) lists and develop their TMDL programs. Finally, in 1996, EPA convened a formal advisory committee to recommend ways to strengthen the TMDL program generally.

The Advisory Committee Recommendations

In the mid-1990s, EPA found itself under increasing pressure from environmental groups and continuing resistance from most states and point source and non-point source industries with regard to the TMDL program. In an effort to break that logjam, EPA formed an advisory committee under the Federal Advisory Committee Act (FACA) composed of 20 members representing point source and non-point source industries, state, local, and tribal governments, the environmental community and others. This TMDL advisory committee, on which I served, issued a report in the summer of 1998 containing over 150 recommendations on ways to strengthen and improve the TMDL program. Most of those recommendations were based on consensus agreement among the members of the committee, but others did not receive the support of the full committee, and there were several important issues on which the committee could not agree at all. . . .

I believe the most important lesson to be derived from the efforts of EPA's TMDL advisory committee was that representatives of the various constituencies most affected by and concerned with the TMDL program agreed, for the most part, on a series of recommendations for strengthening that program. NO single member agreed with all recommendations, and there were important issues left unresolved. But this was an important demonstration of how government, industry, environmentalists and others could work together to develop better ways of solving long-standing and important environmental problems.

The Proposed Rules

In August of [1999], EPA finally published in the Federal Register proposed rules intended to clarify and strengthen the TMDL program. The proposed rules retain the fundamental approaches of the TMDL program—especially the primary role reserved to the states—but add significant detail about how states should manage the program. The one change that has brought the most attention is the proposed requirement of an implementation plan as part of the TMDL-based watershed recovery plan that states submit to EPA for review and approval. While the environmental community is not of one mind about the merits of the proposed rules, I believe the inclusion of an implementation plan alone could have the effect of converting what has largely been a paper exercise to one that has some chance of actually succeeding in cleaning up the nation's worst polluted waters.

In light of intense criticism from virtually all quarters, I think it's safe to say that no constituency is satisfied with EPA's proposed rules. Indeed, some consider that a sign that EPA has struck a reasonable balance among competing interests, though the only real measure of these rules is whether they would speed the clean-up our nation's polluted waters. Environmentalists generally are concerned that the schedules are too long and contain no deadlines; that the offset provision, despite some strengths, contains loopholes that could render it meaningless and ineffective; that the failure to require TMDLs for waters impaired only by "pollution," such as conditions of reduced instream flow, condemns such waters to continued degradation, and that the petition process is unnecessary and destructive of what little trust has been earned on this issue. State governments, even those with sincere commitments to cleaning up polluted waters, are concerned about the resources necessary to develop and implement TMDLs, including for increased monitoring and other data collection. Point source industries and municipalities are concerned that they will have to shoulder an unfair burden by reducing their discharges even further than they have already, and with the potential impact that limiting new or additional discharges might have on economic growth and development. Non-point sources fear the introduction of federal regulatory controls, though EPA has gone to great lengths to explain that no such additional controls are proposed, with the possible exception for previously unregulated point source discharges from forestry operations. . . .

Emphasizing Voluntary Approaches

Despite the uproar about EPA's supposed extension of federal regulatory authority over non-point source activities, that is simply not the case. The proposed rules retain the existing approach whereby states are primarily responsible for securing non-point source reductions where necessary to meet water quality standards. Some states have chosen approaches that depend on regulations to varying degrees; most will continue to emphasize voluntary approaches, primarily educational and cost-sharing in nature. As long as the state's chosen approach actually succeeds in restoring and maintaining water quality, there need be no further debate about federal intrusion because the state will be allowed to implement its chosen approach. When a state's preferred approach falls short, however, then EPA will be justified in requiring more from that state. Even in the worst case, when a state walks away from its obligations or proves incapable of dealing effectively with non-point source problems, EPA will bring no new regulatory authority to the table beyond the minor example discussed above.

Getting to the Nonpoint

According to the U.S. Environmental Protection Agency (EPA), after nearly 30 years of the Clean Water Act, 40 percent of U.S. waters remain polluted—largely by nonpoint source pollution. The situation won't improve unless we "get to the nonpoint" with more scientific data, more targeted funding, tougher laws and nonpoint source enforcement. For the environment and the economy, we must act decisively and comprehensively to stem the flow of nonpoint source pollution.

Association of Metropolitan Sewerage Agencies, "Clean Water . . . We've Got the Point. Now Let's Get to the Nonpoint," 2001.

I suspect the real concern that non-point sources have with the TMDL program is that they are included at all. . . . However, Section 303(d), while not a model of clarity, does require TDMLs for all waters for which the first round of technology-based, point source pollution controls are not sufficient to meet any applicable water quality standard. It would seem axiomatic that such waters include those impaired by non-point source activities, where technology-based point source controls could not possibly succeed in meeting water quality standards. It would also be more logical and efficient for non-point sources to be included in this comprehensive approach to restoring water quality, as EPA has long contended. Subsequent congressional efforts that focused more specifically on non-point source problems, such as Section 319 of the Clean Water Act, in no way detract from this position.

The Authority to Act

There is also significant concern about whether EPA has the legal authority to require implementation plans as part of the TMDL submitted for review and approval under Section 303(d), as opposed to requiring them as part of an occasionally updated continuing planning process under Section 303(e). Regardless of the fact that the continuing planning process under Section 303(e) is one of the few Clean Water Act programs that is even less effective than the TMDL program, it simply makes more sense to relate the numeric reductions represented by the calculation of a TMDL to detailed descriptions of how those reductions will be achieved, as required by the proposed implementation plan, as part of the same process, undertaken at the same time, and reviewed together to determine the likelihood of success. Section 303(d) (1) (C) requires that TMDLs "be established at a level necessary to implement the applicable water quality standards. . . ." Without the implementation plan, recent history has demonstrated that numeric calculations alone, even though they might meet the current regulatory definition of a TMDL, rarely succeed in establishing compliance with water quality standards. EPA's proposal to require implementation plans as a necessary component of TMDLs is both authorized by the statute and sound public policy.

Finally, virtually all parties, including EPA, are concerned about having the resources to develop and implement TMDLs across the nation. Proposed increases in EPA's TMDL budget and other federal funds for non-point source programs will certainly help. I believe, however, that Congress will have to recognize that the restoration of water quality across this country, so strongly supported by the American people, is unlikely to be achieved without this additional funding and perhaps more. Indeed, I was gratified to see the leadership of [Congress] recognize the need for additional funding for the Clean Water Act in a December 1999 letter to the President.

I believe that EPA's proposed rules represent the best chance of moving this program forward. Without implementation plans, TMDLs have proven largely to be a waste of taxpayer money. More importantly, they have been largely ineffective in restoring our most polluted waters to healthy condition. Our best hope for attaining the lofty goals of the 1972 Clean Water Act, restoring the chemical, physical, and biological integrity of our nation's waters, is in moving forward with a TMDL program that has some chance of actually succeeding. EPA's proposed rules represent a significant step in that direction.[2]

2. The Environmental Protection Agency withdrew its July 2000 Total Maximum Daily Load (TMDL) rule on March 19, 2003. While the old TMDL rule remains in effect, environmental groups continue to claim that stricter rules are necessary to control nonpoint source pollution.

"Almost all states are utilizing existing laws, regulations, strategies, and programs to address water quality concerns."

Federal Nonpoint Source Pollution Laws Should Not Be Strengthened

National Association of State Departments of Agriculture

Current rules that govern the Total Maximum Daily Load (TMDL), the amount of water pollution a source may discharge, effectively control water pollution, maintains the National Association of State Departments of Agriculture (NASDA) in the following viewpoint. Stricter rules would exceed federal authority, NASDA argues, and would hamper successful state programs already in place. For example, NASDA claims, strict requirements would harm efforts by farmers and landowners who are already using proven techniques that limit water pollution. NASDA represents the state departments of agriculture in the development of public policies that support the agricultural industry.

As you read, consider the following questions:

1. According to NASDA, what programs have farmers and ranchers participated in that have resulted in water quality gains?
2. What are some of the best management practices used by agricultural producers and other landowners, in the author's opinion?

National Association of State Departments of Agriculture, "Written Statement of the National Association of State Departments of Agriculture Submitted to the House Transportation and Infrastructure Committee, Subcommittee on Water Resources and Environment on Environmental Protection Agency's (EPA) Proposed Regulations for Total Maximum Daily Loads (TMDLs)," www.nasda.org, February 15, 2000.

The National Association of State Departments of Agriculture (NASDA) is pleased to submit the following written testimony regarding the Environmental Protection Agency's (EPA) proposed regulations on Total Maximum Daily Loads (TMDLs)[1] and water quality management.

NASDA, representing the commissioners, secretaries, directors of the state departments of agriculture in the fifty states and four territories, supports the protection of the environment and the wise use of our natural resources. American agriculture is dependent upon continued access to clean water, air, and fertile land for its viability.

Examining Major Concerns

The proposed TMDL rulemaking will have a significant impact on agricultural activities and individual farm and ranch operations nationwide. Following is a description of our major concerns that we hope the Subcommittee will fully explore:

- The TMDL rule greatly exceeds EPA's statutory authority under the Clean Water Act (CWA) to regulate nonpoint source pollution without an expressed congressional mandate to do so.
- The TMDL rule jeopardizes successful state and federal voluntary, incentive-based nonpoint source management programs.
- The TMDL rule significantly expands "command and control" regulatory mandates and does not give states flexibility to implement alternative, or "functionally equivalent" strategies.
- The TMDL rule fails to recognize the substantial state resources needed to address nonpoint source pollution including financial and technical assistance, scientific data, monitoring, and research.

Disrupting Successful Nonpoint Source Programs

NASDA is extremely concerned that the proposed TMDL rules will disrupt and undermine existing state and federal

---

1. The TMDL program, a part of the Clean Water Act, calculates the maximum amount of a pollutant that a water body can receive and still meet water quality standards, and allocates that amount to the pollutant's sources.

nonpoint source programs and greatly diminish pollution reduction opportunities in the agricultural sector. The Clean
Water Act (CWA) contains valuable provisions for nonpoint
source management under Section 319 and Section 208.
However, the CWA does not stand alone in protecting
America's water from nonpoint source pollution. Farmers
and ranchers have provided tremendous water quality gains
through their participation in programs established under
the 1985, 1990 and 1996 Farm Bills. These programs include
the Environmental Quality Incentive Program (EQIP), the
Conservation Reserve Program (CRP), and the Wetlands
Reserve Program (WRP). Most states have developed—and
are implementing—aggressive nonpoint source programs to
protect water quality, including nutrient management and
permitting programs. Agricultural producers and other
landowners have integrated complex systems of best management practices (BMPs) into their planning and operations.
Today, millions of farmland acres are protected by conservation buffers, grassed waterways, contour strips planting, conservation tillage, and other BMPs. The benefits are being
seen in cleaner water, improved wildlife habitat, and the protection of land from soil and wind erosion.

EPA's proposed rule fails to allow states the flexibility to
build on this progress. Instead, EPA's TMDL proposals substantially rewrite implementation of the Clean Water Act
with prescriptive requirements, short deadlines, new and additional layers of planning, implementation, and oversight.
This is counterproductive. Revisions in the TMDL program
should allow for its use where it can be most effective in solving water quality problems. It should not simply replace or
inappropriately conflict with other long-standing CWA and
nonpoint source programs. TMDLs are only one of many
useful planning tools for states to evaluate environmental
risks on agricultural lands and develop and implement plans
to address those risks. For example, states could effectively
use TMDLs as the initial basis to direct increased monitoring and reallocation of resources, so that we know which
management practices and investments should be supported
through financial, technical, educational, or research assistance. This will help us produce more environmental bene-

fits. Instead, it appears that EPA is attempting to leverage a potentially good planning tool into a comprehensive and rigid regulatory program without providing the data and science to make it work. It makes no sense for federal programs to duplicate the state's efforts or require us to change course now and dismantle existing structures that are successfully working.

A Need for Flexibility and Incentives

States must have the flexibility to implement their own existing or new "functionally equivalent" strategies that achieve national environmental objectives. As we noted above, almost all states are utilizing existing laws, regulations, strategies, and programs to address water quality concerns associated with agricultural production. States are aggressively pursuing and expanding resource conservation efforts to minimize agricultural nonpoint source pollution. Significant environmental improvements have been achieved. In many cases, this has occurred without legislation or regulation at the federal level. We strongly believe that alternative or functionally equivalent state strategies may yield more environmental progress and a greater commitment to implementation of nonpoint management programs. EPA's approach under the TMDL proposal only expands a "command and control" regime of new regulations and requirements. Providing states with the ability of using a menu of options will allow us to build on existing programs, authorities, and strategies that deal effectively with agricultural runoff. It does not make sense or sound public policy for the federal government to promote economic environmental partnerships with farmers on one level, then saddle them with increased regulatory requirements and burdens. For example, instead of calling for regulation if an initial round of BMPs do not reach water quality goals within a specified timeframe, a second round of upgraded land management practices that are most likely to be adopted by landowners on a voluntary basis, given adequate technical and financial assistance, should follow. Many farmers and ranchers actively seek opportunities to manage their land to support environmental objectives. Many more would do so if provided with the right incentives and support. The proposed TMDL rule wrongly attempts to micro-manage state conservation planning, and does nothing to encourage farmer participation or create opportunities for improving water quality protection.

Setting Unattainable Standards

Congress elected to treat point and nonpoint sources distinctly for good cause. Congress realized that because of its diffuse and complicated nature, nonpoint source pollution did not lend itself to rigid point source-type controls. Rather, nonpoint source pollution had to be managed through flexible standards. Watershed managers and nonpoint source professionals are well aware of this problem. Farmers and ranchers can't control the rain! But nonpoint source TMDLs expect them to. All four components of the term—Total, Maximum, Daily and Load—imply a constant, engineered and controllable environment. Many environmental groups have long argued that a TMDL has to be just what it says it is—an enforceable DAILY load. For agriculture, this means that farmers are in jeopardy of breaking the law any time a significant rainfall event occurs. Such an outcome is preposterous. As Congress recognized in 1972, while nonpoint sources can be managed "to the extent feasible," they cannot be expected to meet any quantifiable daily load limitations.

John Barrett, statement before the Senate Committee on Environment and Public Works, May 18, 2000.

Improvements in water quality in watersheds that are impaired by agricultural activities will also require the full cooperation of agricultural communities. Proceeding with a strategy that is based on heavy-handed mandates will not foster cooperation. Rather, we fear it will result in litigation, and only delay further water quality improvements. Our experience has shown that successful environmental efforts have been obtained where the activities are voluntary, use partnerships in a team approach, and meet the specific needs of each area. Agricultural producers are willing to do their part in promoting and adopting good management practices that will protect water quality. Any revisions to the TMDL program should emphasize cooperative—rather than regulatory—approaches to nonpoint source pollution reduction, and be led by conservation districts and watershed partnerships. This will allow states to move forward in addressing agricultural nonpoint source pollution priorities.

A Need for Financial Resources and Improved Water Quality Data

The state departments of agriculture want to emphasize the importance of financial resources and technical assistance. We have often stressed the need for consistent and increased federal funding for nonpoint source programs. Over the past two decades, federal agencies have seriously under-invested in efforts to control and abate nonpoint pollution problems. Although nonpoint source programs have historically received only about one or two percent as much federal funding as point source control programs, they have nonetheless resulted in significant reductions in soil erosion and runoff of agricultural stormwater. Further progress in achieving water quality goals will require a much greater federal commitment to adequate funding. We are particularly concerned that EPA's economic analysis provided in the proposed TMDL rule is inaccurate and inadequate. The state water control administrators have estimated that $5 billion in new costs will be needed, not including costs to the private sector, for states to comply with the proposed TMDL requirements. Clearly, EPA should complete a comprehensive cost analysis before proceeding with the proposed rule.[2]

NASDA welcomes the administration's recent announcement to seek $1.3 billion in the FY2001 budget for conservation programs to help family farmers take steps to protect water quality and the environment. This new budget initiative is the correct approach to solving water quality problems because it recognizes the importance of flexible, incentive-based, and site-specific programs. It provides a tremendous opportunity to accelerate agricultural conservation practices, and establish working partnerships with key agricultural stakeholders. This is especially true since unlike some busi-

2. The Environmental Protection Agency withdrew its July 2000 Total Maximum Daily Load (TMDL) rule on March 19, 2003. While the old TMDL rule remains in effect, environmental groups continue to claim that stricter rules are necessary to control nonpoint source pollution.

nesses, utilities, or government, farmers and ranchers cannot raise the value of their products to offset the costs of best management practices or regulatory requirements. It is unrealistic to expect them to participate without adequate financial and technical assistance. These new conservation initiatives should be fully funded, implemented, and evaluated before additional "command and control" strategies, such as the federal TMDL regulations, are promulgated.

State departments of agriculture represent a tremendous asset that can be of considerable assistance to the country's effort to create a successful working partnership between agriculture and the environment. NASDA appreciates your leadership in holding oversight hearings on the TMDL rulemaking and the impact it will have on farm and ranch operations. We stand ready to work with Congress, EPA, and USDA to develop strategies and policies that will focus on environmental results to achieve our mutual water quality goals.

> "[Raising the CAFE standards] could . . .
> cut 240 million tons of carbon dioxide
> pollution each year."

Stricter Fuel Standards Will Reduce Pollution

Rachel Filippini

Raising Corporate Average Fuel Economy (CAFE) standards to thirty-six miles per gallon for both passenger cars and light trucks would substantially reduce air pollution, argues Rachel Filippini in the following viewpoint. In 1975 Congress set CAFE standards to increase the fuel efficiency of passenger vehicles, Filippini explains. Unfortunately, gas-guzzling sport-utility vehicles (SUVs) and light trucks are held to lower fuel efficiency standards than are cars, and since these vehicles now make up a large share of the passenger-vehicle market, auto emissions have increased. These vehicles should be subject to strict CAFE standards and taxes that encourage fuel economy, he maintains. Filippini is an executive assistant with Group Against Smog and Pollution.

As you read, consider the following questions:

1. In Filippini's opinion, why is transferring the responsibility of raising CAFE standards to the National Highway Traffic Safety Administration a bad move?
2. Where does a vast majority of the fuel savings come from when developing more fuel-efficient vehicles, in the author's view?
3. According to the author, how much smog-forming exhaust does the average truck on the road emit?

Rachel Filippini, "Better Fuel Economy Standards Needed," *GASPHotline*, Winter 2003. Copyright © 2003 by *GASPHotline*. Reproduced by permission.

For the majority of us, driving is probably the most polluting activity we do each day. For every gallon of gasoline consumed, approximately 24 lbs. of global warming pollutants are released into the air. Cars and light trucks alone emit 20% of the nation's human-produced carbon dioxide, the chief heat-trapping gas blamed for global warming, and they consume approximately 8 million barrels of oil every day. Can anything be done to help remedy the situation?

Improving Fuel Economy

In 1975, in response to the Arab oil embargo of 1973–74 and the subsequent tripling in price of crude oil, the Energy Policy and Conservation Act established Corporate Average Fuel Economy (CAFE) standards for passenger cars, for model years 1978–80 and 1985 and thereafter. The CAFE standards called for essentially a doubling in new car fleet fuel economy, establishing a standard of 18 mpg in model year 1978 and rising to 27.5 mpg by 1985. They also established fuel economy standards for light duty trucks, beginning at 17.2 mpg in 1979 and . . . 20.7 mpg [as of 2003]. CAFE standards are applied on a fleet-wide basis for each manufacturer (i.e., the fuel economy ratings for a manufacturer's entire line of passenger cars must average at least 27.5 mpg for the manufacturer to comply with the standard). Currently the passenger automobile standard is set at 27.5 mpg; it has not increased since the 1986 model year. Light trucks, a classification that also includes sport utility vehicles (SUVs) and minivans, have a mere 20.7 mpg standard.

Can raising CAFE standards really make that much of a difference? If the CAFE standards were raised to 36 mpg for both passenger cars and light trucks, as a nation we could save one million barrels of oil per day, as much as the United States now imports from Iraq and Kuwait combined. We could also cut 240 million tons of carbon dioxide pollution each year. A proposal to do this very thing, giving manufacturers until model year 2015, was made in February of 2002 by Senators John Kerry (D-MA) and John McCain (R-AZ). However, on March 13, 2002, the Senate voted (62-38) for an amendment instead offered by Senator Carl Levin (D-MI) and Christopher Bond (R-MO). Their competing amendment would eliminate existing fuel efficiency language from the Senate energy bills and transfer responsibility for raising CAFE standards to the Department of Transportation's National Highway Traffic Safety Administration (NHTSA). According to the U.S. Public Interest Research Group, this was a bad move, since in the last decade NHTSA increased fuel economy standards for light trucks by a meager 0.5 mpg and never acted to increase the standards for cars. With the CAFE standards effectively frozen, the actual fuel economy of our nation's automotive fleet is falling now, as cars coming off the road are more efficient than the new models coming on. "Auto industry resistance and congressional inertia have resulted in a 21-year low in the fuel economy of new vehicles sold" [the Union of Concerned Scientists write].

The Safety Question

Many opponents of increasing the CAFE standards argue that the standards make cars less safe, because higher mileage vehicles are generally lighter than lower mileage vehicles, providing less protection to drivers and passengers in crashes. It is not that simple. According to testimony given to Congress by David Nemtzow, President of Alliance to Save Energy, weight reduction in more fuel efficient vehicles provided only 15 percent of the doubling of fuel economy that occurred between 1975–1986. The vast majority of the savings came from the incorporation of advanced transmissions, drag-reduction techniques, exhaust controls, lighter-weight materials of equal strength, and other technical measures that increased miles per gallon in ways that cannot be construed to affect safety. In July 2001, the National Research Council released a report stating that automakers could meet a 37 mpg fuel economy standard phased in over 10 to 15 years without compromising safety or industry profits.

The SUV Trend

As you've probably noticed, there has been a growing trend towards owning SUVs. The increasing market share of these vehicles, along with their lower average fuel economy, has contributed to the lowering of the overall average fuel economy since the mid-1980s. In 1985, SUVs accounted for only 2% of new vehicle sales. SUVs now account for 25% of new vehicles sold, and sales continue to climb. Unfortunately, this new trendy automobile may be detrimental to the environment. These off-road vehicles that rarely leave the pavement are characterized as light trucks under the law; therefore, the CAFE standard is 20.7 mpg. This is an average for all light trucks, which is why it is possible to have SUVs on the road that only achieve 12 mpg. Some SUVs are so behemoth that they can no longer be classified as light trucks and are not subject to any kind of fuel economy standards. The average truck on the road emits 47% more smog-forming exhaust and 43% more global warming pollution than the average car. However, even light trucks and SUVs can take advantage of technologies to assist them in being more fuel-efficient. For instance, a combination of streamlining, reduced tire rolling resistance, engine improvements and optimized transmission could all help increase fuel economy.

The Gas Guzzler Tax

Millions of inefficient light trucks (including SUVs) are used as passenger vehicles, yet they are NOT subject to the Gas Guzzler Tax (ranging from $1000 to $7700) that is imposed on inefficient cars. The Energy Tax Act of 1978 established the Gas Guzzler Tax on the sale of new model year vehicles whose fuel economy fails to meet certain statutory levels. The Gas Guzzler Tax applies to cars, not trucks, and is collected by the IRS. According to the American Council for an Energy Efficient Economy, applying the Gas Guzzler Tax to all gas-guzzling passenger vehicles, including trucks and SUVs, would "pull up" the bottom end of the vehicle fleet and generate tax revenue that could be used to reimburse the government for any incentives they may offer to buyers of high-efficiency vehicles. The original CAFE law provided a different standard for light trucks because they were relatively few in number and traveled fewer miles than passenger cars, due to the assumptions that they were generally engaged in commercial activities that set them apart from personal-use vehicles. However, the use of many light trucks has changed. EPA has found that light trucks are largely used

'We're leaving, Bunty! They allow smoking!!'

Williams. © 2004 by Mike Williams. Reproduced by permission.

as passenger vehicles and log similar distances. Shouldn't the CAFE standards reflect this fact?

Recently a bi-partisan bill, introduced by Senators Joe Lieberman (D-CT) and John McCain (R-AZ), is attempting to curb global warming by establishing a market-based trading system in greenhouse gas emissions.[1] The McCain/Lieberman bill would set a nationwide cap limiting pollution from major sources in the industrial, commercial, electricity, and transportation fuel sectors, which together are responsible for nearly 80% of U.S. emissions. This legislation followed news that 2002 was the second warmest summer on record. The ten warmest years have all occurred since 1987, with nine of them happening since 1990. According to the legislation, automakers could earn credits that they could sell to other companies if they exceeded the CAFE standards by more than 20%. Companies would have the choice of reducing their emissions to reduce their required allowances or purchasing other companies' allowances to cover their continued emissions. Any companies that voluntarily under-

1. The Senate rejected the bill in October 2003.

took efforts to reduce their greenhouse gases would receive credit for those actions.

It is evident that leaving this matter in the hands of President [George W.] Bush would not be wise. Recently the administration leaked an agency proposal that, on the surface, calls for a very small increase in the fuel economy of SUVs and other light trucks. However, on closer analysis, with the many loopholes that the auto industry enjoys, the oil savings would be negligible. In fact, what the administration is proposing is actually less aggressive than what the automakers have said they would voluntarily do by 2005.

What Can You Do?

The choice of the vehicle that you drive has a major impact on the environment. Not only do you have to consider the fuel economy of the vehicle you drive, but also the tailpipe emissions. Choosing a low-emission, fuel-efficient vehicle can reduce the environmental impact of driving. There are many practical driving tips that can reduce your contribution to air pollution:

- First and foremost, limit driving: use public transportation, carpool, bike, walk, combine errands, etc.
- Avoid high speeds; high speed driving increases fuel use and emissions.
- Keep your vehicle well-tuned.
- Drive an alternative vehicle or alternatively fueled vehicle.
- Make sure tires are properly inflated; keeping your tires properly inflated saves fuel by reducing the amount of drag your engine must overcome.
- Do not overfill or top off your gasoline tank.
- Do not refuel on high ozone days; try to refuel after dark.
- Drive smoothly and avoid lengthy idling. Letting your engine idle for more than a minute burns more fuel than turning off the engine and restarting it.
- Promptly repair any leaks in your vehicle's air conditioning system.
- When possible, park in the shade to minimize fuel evaporation and keep your car cooler in the summer.

When shopping for a new automobile, look for the one that is least polluting and most fuel-efficient that will meet your needs. Recognize that not all fuel-efficient vehicles are better for the environment; for instance, some powered by diesel fuel can have high efficiency but dirty emissions. Increasing the number of diesel vehicles on the road offers only modest potential reductions in global-warming pollution, but it poses a significant risk to air quality.

"The CAFE standards save very little gasoline, increase car buyers' costs and lower their benefits, [and] increase pollution and auto fatalities."

Stricter Fuel Standards Will Not Reduce Pollution

Andrew N. Kleit

Raising the Corporate Average Fuel Economy (CAFE) standards will not reduce pollution, claims Andrew N. Kleit in the following viewpoint. In fact, he argues, increasing a car's fuel efficiency actually increases pollution. Emissions are determined by the number of miles driven, Kleit maintains, and because increased fuel efficiency makes gas less expensive, people drive more, increasing air pollution. Kleit is professor of energy and environmental economics at Pennsylvania State University.

As you read, consider the following questions:
1. According to Kleit, how do foreign automakers view CAFE fines?
2. How do CAFE standards affect the production of "gas-guzzlers," in the author's view?
3. What does the author suggest would be a better way to reduce energy consumption than CAFE standards?

L ast March [2002], the U.S. Senate considered a proposal by Sen. John Kerry (D-Mass.) to raise the Corporate Average Fuel Economy (CAFE) standards for cars and light trucks by 50 percent. Kerry and other proponents of stricter standards had the support of a July 2001 report by the National Research Council (NRC) that called for significantly higher standards, as well as the backing of many major newspapers. The [September 11, 2001, terrorist attacks] and the subsequent resurgence of violence and political uncertainty in the Mideast added to the momentum in favor of new fuel efficiency standards. But a coalition of Republicans and auto-state Democrats defeated the Kerry measure by a decisive and surprising 62-38 vote.

To the casual observer, the decision may have seemed a defeat of the public interest by special interests. In fact, it was a victory for economic common sense. As many economists and other policy experts have argued, the CAFE standards save very little gasoline, increase car buyers' costs and lower their benefits, increase pollution and auto fatalities, and shift revenue away from U.S. automakers to foreign firms. Instead of raising the fuel efficiency standards, policymakers would better address any externalities associated with gasoline by raising the gas tax.

A Brief History

The CAFE program, enacted in 1975, required all manufacturers selling more than 10,000 autos per year in the United States to have sales-weighted fuel economy of 19.0 miles per gallon in 1978. That meant that all of the new cars that an automaker sold had to average 19 mpg, though individual models could have gas mileages below that level. Under the law, the mileage standard increased to 27.5 mpg in 1985, and it currently remains at that level.

The CAFE law divides an automaker's cars into foreign and domestic fleets. It also offered a different standard for light trucks (pickup trucks, sport-utility vehicles, and minivans)—a concession that seemed insignificant in 1975 because those vehicles comprised only a small percentage of the total number of vehicles on the road. However, that concession has become increasingly significant in recent years as light truck sales—buoyed by the wildly popular sport-utility vehicle—now comprise nearly half of all U.S. auto sales. The National Highway Transportation Safety Administration, using authority granted it through CAFE, currently requires a 20.7-mpg fleet-efficiency standard for light trucks, but the agency is considering raising that standard.

Compliance. If a manufacturer does not comply with the CAFE standards, it is subject to a civil fine of $55 per car/mpg. For example, if a manufacturer produces one million cars with a sales-weighted mpg of 26.5 mpg, that firm could be subject to a fine of $55 per car/mpg × 1 million cars × 1 mpg, or $55 million.

Foreign automakers view the fine as a tax. Thus, BMW and Mercedes-Benz, for example, have routinely paid CAFE fines. In contrast, American firms view the standards as binding because their lawyers have advised them that, if they violate CAFE, they would be liable for civil damages in stockholder suits. The fear of civil suit is so strong that even Chrysler, which is owned by the German firm Daimler-Benz, will not violate the limits. Because the "shadow tax" of the CAFE constraint (the cost of complying with the standards rather than paying the fine) can be much more than $55 per car/mpg, the effects of CAFE standards are much larger on U.S. automakers than foreign firms. . . .

The Problems with CAFE

Ignoring concerns over feasibility, CAFE proponents claim that increasing the fuel efficiency standards has the added advantage of creating net benefits apart from any reduction in the external cost of gasoline use. The NRC report goes so far as to assert that higher standards would actually pay for themselves, with the increased costs more than offset by reduced fuel consumption—yet another "free lunch" from Washington, D.C.

Contrary to those claims, it appears that stricter standards would save very little gasoline. There are three basic reasons for that:

- CAFE has only a limited effect on the production of "gas-guzzlers."
- CAFE leads to increased driving.

- CAFE keeps older cars with lower gas mileage on the road.

Gas-guzzlers. The CAFE standards affect the mix of vehicles produced by a manufacturer, but not the overall production of any particular type of car. That is important to remember because, as explained earlier, domestic firms will feel constrained by the new standards but foreign firms will not. The constrained U.S. firms will be forced to increase their fuel efficiency, leaving an undersupply in the large-car market. In turn, foreign firms will move into that market and begin producing vehicles with lower fuel efficiency. Though the cars will have a slightly higher price because of CAFE fines, they likely will still appeal to consumers, so the overall mix of cars being sold will not change nearly as much as what CAFE proponents expect.

Foreign automakers stand to draw a lot of profits away from U.S. firms if stricter CAFE standards are adopted. Honda and Toyota, for example, have fleet averages now that likely would satisfy any new standards that Congress might pass, hence the automakers would have no disincentive to try for a larger share of the U.S. large-car market. (In fact, they may feel they need to move into that market because U.S. automakers will be moving into the small-car market.) Even if the foreign automakers' fleet averages would not satisfy the new standards, the automakers likely would pay the relatively small mileage fines in order to have a larger share of the market.

More driving. CAFE standards may reduce the consumption of fuel per mile, but they also increase the overall amount of driving. Because the standards lower the per-mile cost of operating a car, drivers have less financial incentive to drive less. Vehicle use is just like any other market in which demand is responsive to price: A decrease in cost remits in an increase in aggregate use. The latest estimates are that for every 10 percent increase in fuel efficiency, people increase their driving by two percent. Those trends indicate, again, that the fuel savings from tighter CAFE standards will be less than what proponents believe.

Old cars. By raising the cost of new cars, CAFE standards provide a disincentive for old-car owners to trade in their lower-gas-mileage vehicles for new, more-efficient ones. That, in turn, increases gasoline consumption by older cars because they will be staying on the road instead of being taken to the scrap yards. So, yet again, stricter CAFE standards will have less of a gas-saving effect than what proponents claim.

Other problems. CAFE standards not only save very little gasoline, they increase air pollutants such as volatile organic compounds (VOC), oxides of nitrogen (NO_x), and carbon monoxide (CO). The increases occur because the standards do not alter a car's grams/mile of emissions and thus do nothing to alter pollution levels directly. Because the pollution from a car is a direct function of the number of miles it is driven, and people in more fuel-efficient vehicles drive more, the net result from an increase in CAFE standards is an increase in automobile pollutants.

Increased CAFE standards also result in more auto fatalities. As the NRC panel conceded in its report, compliance with stricter standards means that automakers lighten their cars. Lighter, smaller cars, in turn, mean more fatalities from automobile accidents.

Finally, CAFE standards are, in large part, unworkable because demand can shift much more quickly than a manufacturer's ability to alter the fuel use of its vehicles. For example, it would take a firm three to five years to re-engineer its cars so that, at current demand levels, the fleet would satisfy a new standard. But consumers can change their buying habits in an extremely short period of time and can buy a mix of cars very different than what automakers expected. Automakers, through no fault of their own, could face short-run CAFE problems that they could address only through "mix-shifting"—selling fewer large cars and more small cars by raising prices on the former and lowering them on the latter. Because mix-shifting annoys consumers and reduces industry employment, the government has little choice but to grant the automakers relief, or else the politicians will permit serious unemployment and economic harm.

These considerations further indicate that the benefits of new CAFE standards will be less, and the negative effects more, than what proponents believe.

Better Mileage, Worse Air

	Change Under 3MPG Increase in CAFE Standards	Change Under 50% Increase in CAFE Standards
% Change in VOC Emissions	1.64%	2.30%
% Change in NO_x Emissions	1.80%	3.82%
% Change in CO Emissions	1.86%	4.97%
Change in Gasoline Consumption (billion gallons)	−5.091 (−7.15%)	−15.994 (−22.04%)
Average Cost of reducing Gasoline Externality	$0.58	$1.68
Marginal Cost of reducing Gasoline Externality	$1.06	$3.93

Andrew N. Kleit, *Regulation*, Fall 2002.

The Effects on Automakers

On behalf of General Motors, I created a model of the impact of stricter CAFE standards on domestic and foreign automakers. I assumed that the relevant period is the "long-run," so as to allow for the development of new technologies that would assist firms in meeting the stricter standards. As part of the model, I considered two different proposals for new CAFE standards: the 3-mpg increase proposed by Vice President Dick Cheney's energy task force and the 50-percent increase proposed by Sen. Kerry. For my cost-benefit analysis, I adopted the NRC assumption that the level of externality associated with a gallon of gasoline is 26¢, despite my reservations about that figure. . . .

Cheney proposal. I found that increasing the CAFE standards by 3 mpg would reduce annual profits at General Motors by $433 million, at Ford by $455 million, and at Chrysler by $236 million. Total losses to U.S. automakers would amount to $1.124 billion. In contrast, foreign manufacturers would see an increase in profits of $260 million.

With respect to consumers, losses are measured in terms of the economic concept of "consumer surplus." For example, assume a consumer values a car for $20,000, and is able to purchase it for $18,000. That consumer would gain $2,000 in consumer surplus. If CAFE standards make that car unavailable and the consumer chooses not to purchase a car, the new standards would have caused a loss of $2,000 in consumer surplus for that consumer. If the fuel efficiency standards were to be increased 3 mpg, I estimate that U.S. consumer surplus would decline $1.841 billion.

Emissions of all three "criteria" pollutants would increase relative to emissions if the CAFE standards remained unchanged. Increasing the standards by 3 MPG would increase VOC emissions by 1.64 percent, NO_x emissions by 1.80 percent, and CO emissions by 1.86 percent. The new standards would result in a decrease in consumption of 5.091 billion gallons, or about 7.15 percent of fleet consumption. The marginal cost of a gallon of gasoline saved would be $1.06.

Kerry proposal. Increasing the CAFE standards by 50 percent would cause far more harm to the economy. I estimate that passage of the Kerry proposal would have reduced annual profits at General Motors by $3.824 billion, at Ford by $3.423 billion, and at Chrysler by $1.959 billion. Total losses to U.S. automakers would amount to $9.206 billion. In contrast, foreign manufacturers would see an increase in profits of $4.434 billion. Consumer surplus would decline $17.603 billion.

Emissions of all three "criteria" pollutants would increase above what would occur if the CAFE standards remained unchanged. Increasing fuel efficiency as proposed would increase VOC emissions by 1.87 percent, NO_x emissions by 3.41 percent, and CO emissions by 4.57 percent. The new standards would result in a decrease in consumption of 14.690 billion gallons, or about 20.6 percent of fleet consumption. The marginal cost of a gallon of gasoline saved would be $3.93.

Given the estimates generated by my model, what are the costs and benefits of the two CAFE proposals? Let us assume, as the NRC indicates, that the external cost of the consumption of a gallon of gasoline is 26¢ per gallon—which would thus be the benefit from a gallon of gasoline not consumed. My model indicates that the average cost of a 3-mpg increase in fuel standards is 2.2 (58¢ ÷ 26¢) times the benefits. The average cost of a 50-percent increase in the standards is about 6.5 ($1.68 ÷ 26¢) times the benefits. The marginal cost of the Cheney proposal would be 4.1 ($1.06 ÷ 26¢) times the benefits. And the marginal cost of the Kerry proposal is 15.1 ($3.93 ÷ 26¢) times the benefits.

Proponents of stricter CAFE standards, including the authors of the recent NRC report, claim that increasing the CAFE standards is the policy equivalent of a free lunch. But fuel efficiency standards are an extremely poor policy tool. If enforced, they would reduce consumer welfare and motorist safety, harm the environment, and increase the profits of foreign firms. Worst of all, they do not save gasoline very effectively.

If policymakers wish to reduce energy consumption, they should tax gasoline consumption. It is that simple. Unfortunately, altering the CAFE standards is a politically attractive policy to invoke to reduce gasoline consumption's external costs. Because of that attractiveness, there is little debate on the real issues involved in energy consumption.

Periodical Bibliography

The following articles have been selected to supplement the diverse views presented in this chapter.

Rosina M. Bierbaum — "The Bumpy Road to Reduced Carbon Emissions," *Issues in Science and Technology*, Summer 2003.

David Bosch — "Total Maximum Daily Loads: Part Two; Why Are They Necessary? How Will They Impact You?" *Engineering & Technology for a Sustainable World*, March 2003.

Martha Brand — "Can Coal Come Clean?" *Issues in Science and Technology*, Summer 2004.

Congressional Digest — "Fight for Air: The New Debate over Industrial Emissions," March 2003.

Robert M. Cox — "Superfund Destroys a Small Business: Liable for Cleanup Whether Guilty or Not," *PERC Reports*, March 2003.

Tom Davey — "The Cote D'Azur Was Lovely—but Are Ocean Liners Polluters?" *Environmental Science & Engineering*, January 2002.

Pierre Desrochers — "Regulatory Roadblocks to Turning Waste to Wealth," *Freeman: Ideas on Liberty*, September 2003.

Elizabeth Grossman — "A Race to the Top?" *Yes!* Spring 2004.

Sam Kazman — "The Scapegoat Utility Vehicle," *Freeman: Ideas on Liberty*, July 2003.

John L. Kirkwood — "'Clear Skies' Won't Clear the Air," *National Voter*, September/October 2003.

Stuart Lieberman — "Pollution with a Point," *International Real Estate Digest*, December 10, 2000.

Isabel Lyman — "Superfund Destroys a Business," *New American*, January 26, 2004.

Joyce Marcel — "Acid Raindrops Keep Falling on My Head," CommonDreams.org, October 2, 2003.

Jim Motavalli — "Collect Them All!" *E Magazine*, March 2001.

Ralph Nader — "Spinning Wheels—Our Continual Refusal to Raise CAFE Standards," CommonDreams.org, April 12, 2004.

Peter VanDoren and Michael Gough — "Extrinsic Toxic Waste Superfund," *Washington Times*, July 18, 2002.

For Further Discussion

Chapter 1

1. Some authors in this chapter assert that despite measurable improvements, pollution continues to be a problem, and additional measures are needed to protect human health and the environment. Other authors argue that such claims are exaggerated; they cite improvement in the environment as evidence that human innovation will prevent pollution problems in the future. Do you think the authors of this latter view provide sufficient evidence that U.S. industries will develop pollution-reducing innovations on their own, or do you think the pressure of activists is necessary to motivate these innovations? Explain.

2. Stephen Moore claims that America's air and water are cleaner than ever and that economic growth has led to environmental improvement. What other factors do the authors in this chapter claim contribute to improvements in U.S. air and water quality? Explain your answer, citing from the viewpoints.

3. Clive Tesar argues that persistent organic pollutants (POPs) pose a threat to human health. William F. Jasper believes that banning POPs poses a more serious threat than that posed by the POPs themselves. Citing from the texts, explain which viewpoint you find more persuasive.

4. Joe Bower lists many different environmental impacts of light pollution. Which of these threats do you believe is the most serious? Explain.

Chapter 2

1. Authors in this chapter who believe that the public health threat of pollution is exaggerated argue that such claims are based on flawed evidence. What kind of evidence do you think would be sufficient to prove that pollution is a serous threat to human health? Do any of the authors in this chapter provide evidence that you find persuasive? Explain.

2. Kimi Eisele argues that children in communities with high levels of air pollution have higher rates of asthma. Ben Lieberman contends that air pollution has declined, so there must be another explanation for higher asthma rates. Citing from the texts, which of these arguments do you find more convincing?

3. Physicians for Social Responsibility, an organization whose many goals include educating the public about environmental dangers,

contends that mercury contamination is a serious threat to human health. Steven Milloy, a scholar with the Cato Institute, a libertarian think tank that opposes environmental regulations, argues that no evidence proves that consuming typical concentrations of mercury in fish poses a health threat. Citing from the viewpoints, explain how the authors' affiliations are reflected in their viewpoints.

Chapter 3

1. Sam Martin contends that recycling is better for the environment than landfills. Daniel K. Benjamin argues that landfills are better for the environment than recycling. Compare the evidence each author cites to support his claim. Which do you find more persuasive, and why?

2. Friends of the Earth argues that sport-utility vehicles (SUVs) contribute to the air-pollution problem. Nick Gillespie claims that the attack against SUVs is unwarranted and even irrational. He contends that authors attacking SUV drivers rather than the SUV itself lack credibility. Does Friends of the Earth attack SUV drivers? If so, does that make its argument more or less persuasive?

Chapter 4

1. The authors in this chapter disagree on the role that government should play in reducing pollution. What commonalities among the viewpoints that support strict regulation and among those that oppose strict regulation can you find in this chapter? Explain, citing from the viewpoints.

2. Amanda Griscom argues that industries that profit from the production of products that produce toxic waste should be responsible for cleaning up all toxic waste sites, even when they are not directly responsible for the waste. Steven Milloy claims that this is unfair. Based on the arguments presented in the viewpoints, who do you think should be responsible for cleaning up toxic waste? Explain.

3. Richard A. Parrish claims that requiring states to develop stricter rules in order to clean up nonpoint source water pollution is a reasonable request. The National Association of State Departments of Agriculture argues that current regulations are sufficient to protect the water supply and that stricter rules will impede practices already in place. Which argument do you find more persuasive? Explain, citing from the viewpoints.

4. Rachel Filippini believes that raising fuel standards will decrease pollution. Andrew N. Kleit claims that doing so will in fact increase pollution because if people get better gas mileage, they will drive more. What evidence does Filippini cite to support his contention that increased fuel efficiency will reduce pollution? What evidence does Kleit provide to prove that people will drive more? Which evidence do you find more persuasive?

Organizations to Contact

American Council on Science and Health (ACSH)
1995 Broadway, 2nd Floor, New York, NY 10023-5860
(212) 362-7044 • fax: (212) 362-4919
e-mail: acsh@acsh.org • Web site: www.acsh.org
ACSH is a consumer education consortium concerned with, among other topics, issues related to the environment and health. The council publishes editorials, position papers, and books, including "The Mysterious Asthma Increase" and "Who Says PCBs Cause Cancer?" which are available on its Web site.

American Lung Association (ALA)
61 Broadway, 6th Floor, New York, NY 10006
(212) 315-8700
Web site: www.lungusa.org
Founded in 1904 to fight tuberculosis, the American Lung Association currently fights lung disease in all its forms, with special emphasis on asthma, tobacco control, and environmental health. Under the Air Quality link on its Web site the ALA provides articles, fact sheets, and special reports on pollution-related issues, including its yearly "State of the Air."

Bluewater Network
311 California, Suite 510, San Francisco, CA 94104
(415) 544-0790 • fax: (415) 544-0796
e-mail: bluewater@bluewaternetwork.org
Web site: www.bluewaternetwork.org
The Bluewater Network promotes policy changes in government and industry to reduce dependence on fossil fuels and eradicate other root causes of air and water pollution, global warming, and habitat destruction. On its Web site the Bluewater Network publishes fact sheets on specific water pollution issues such as ship emissions, oil spills, and global warming. Articles that are available on the Web site include "Banishing Snowmobiles," "Super-Sized Cruise Ships Leave Wake of Wastes," and "Dirty Diesels."

Cato Institute
1000 Massachusetts Ave. NW, Washington, DC 20001-5403
(202) 842-0200 • fax: (202) 842-3490
e-mail: cato@cato.org • Web site: www.cato.org
The institute is a libertarian public policy research foundation dedicated to limiting the role of government and protecting indi-

vidual liberties. The institute publishes the quarterly magazine *Regulation* and the bimonthly *Cato Policy Report*. It disapproves of EPA regulations, considering them too stringent. On its Web site the institute publishes many of its papers dealing with the environment, including "The Air Pollution Con Game," "Amending Superfund: Reform or Revanche?" and "Our Widespread Faith in Recycling Is Misplaced."

Clear the Air

1200 Eighteenth St. NW, 5th Floor, Washington, DC 20036
(202) 887-1715 • fax: (202) 887-8877
e-mail: info@cleartheair.org • Web site: www.cleartheair.org

Clear the Air, which supports stricter air pollution controls, is a joint project of three leading clean air groups: the Clean Air Task Force, the National Environmental Trust, and the U.S. Public Interest Research Group (PIRG) Education Fund. On its Web site Clear the Air publishes news releases, fact sheets, and reports, including "Pollution on the Rise," "Fishing For Trouble: Mercury Is Making Our Nation's Fish Unsafe To Eat," and "Toxic Neighbors."

Competitive Enterprise Institute (CEI)

1001 Connecticut Ave. NW, Suite 1250, Washington, DC 20036
(202) 331-1010 • fax: (202) 331-0640
e-mail: info@cei.org • Web site: www.cei.org

CEI is a public policy organization dedicated to the principles of free enterprise and limited government. The institute believes that consumers are best helped not by government regulation but by being allowed to make their own choices in a free marketplace and thus supports market-based pollution policies. On its Web site CEI publishes articles, editorials, speeches, and studies, including "Asthma, Roaches, and Regulations," "Superfund Legislation: True Reform or a Hazardous Waste?" and "Foul Water or Foul Science? The EPA Targets America's Farms."

Earth Island Institute (EII)

300 Broadway, Suite 28, San Francisco, CA 94133-3312
(415) 788-3666 • fax: (415) 788-7324
Web site: www.earthisland.org

Founded in 1982 by veteran environmentalist David Brower, EII develops and supports projects that counteract threats to the biological and cultural diversity that sustain the environment. Through education and activism, EII promotes the conservation, preservation, and restoration of the Earth. EII publishes the quarterly *Earth Island Journal*. Recent articles are available on the EII

Web site, including "Breathless in Harlem," "Toxic Toast and Radioactive Raisin Bran," and "Cruise Ships Fail Pollution Tests."

Environmental Protection Agency (EPA)
Ariel Rios Building
1200 Pennsylvania Ave. NW, Washington, DC 20460
(202) 272-0167
Web site: www.epa.gov

The EPA is the federal agency in charge of protecting the environment and controlling pollution. The agency works toward these goals by assisting businesses and local environmental agencies, enacting and enforcing regulations, identifying and fining polluters, and cleaning up polluted sites. On its Web site EPA has links to specific pollution issues, including Acid Rain, the Clean Air Act, Clean Water Act, Hazardous Waste, Superfund, and Recycling. These links include articles, memos, and speeches on a wide variety of pollution-related topics.

Friends of the Earth
1717 Massachusetts Ave. NW, Suite 600, Washington, DC
20036-2002
(877) 843-8687 • fax: (202) 783-0444
e-mail: foe@foe.org • Web site: www.foe.org

Friends of the Earth is a national advocacy organization dedicated to protecting the planet from environmental degradation; preserving biological, cultural, and ethnic diversity; and empowering citizens to have an influential voice in decisions affecting the quality of their environment. It publishes the quarterly *Friends of the Earth Newsmagazine*, recent and archived issues of which are available on its Web site.

GrassRoots Recycling Network (GRRN)
4200 Park Blvd. #290, Oakland, CA 94602
(510) 531-5523 • fax: (510) 531-5523
Web site: www.grrn.org

GRRN's mission is to eliminate the waste of natural and human resources. The network advocates corporate accountability and public policies that eliminate waste and build sustainable communities. The GRRN Web site includes fact sheets, reports, and articles, including "Composting and Organics: Recycling vs. Bioreactors" and "Beyond Recycling: The Zero Waste Solution."

Heritage Foundation
214 Massachusetts Ave. NE, Washington, DC 20002-4999
(800) 544-4843 • (202) 546-4400 • fax: (202) 544-6979
e-mail: pubs@heritage.org • Web site: www.heritage.org

The Heritage Foundation is a conservative think tank that supports free enterprise and limited government. Its researchers criticize EPA overregulation and believe that recycling is an ineffective method of dealing with waste. Its publications, such as the quarterly *Policy Review*, include studies on the uncertainty of global warming and the greenhouse effect. The articles "Keeping It Clean" and "Why the Government's CAFE Standards for Fuel Efficiency Should Be Repealed, Not Increased" are available on its Web site.

International Dark-Sky Association (IDA)
3225 N. First Ave., Tucson, Arizona 85719-2103
(520) 293-3198 • fax: 520-293-3192
e-mail: ida@darksky.org • Web site: www.darksky.org

IDA's goals are to reverse the adverse environmental impact on dark skies by building awareness of the problem of light pollution and the solutions, including quality nighttime lighting. On its Web site IDA publishes fact sheets, slide shows demonstrating the impact of light pollution, and articles, including "Light Pollution: The Neglected Problem."

Natural Resources Defense Council (NRDC)
40 W. Twentieth St., New York, NY 10011
(212) 727-2700
e-mail: proinfo@nrdc.org • Web site: www.nrdc.org

The Natural Resources Defense Council is a nonprofit organization that uses law, science, and more than four hundred thousand members nationwide to protect the planet's wildlife and wild places and to ensure a safe and healthy environment for all living things. On its Web site NRDC provides links to specific pollution-related topics such as Clean Air and Energy, Global Warming, Clean Water and Oceans, and Toxic Chemicals and Health. These links include fact sheets, reports, and articles, including "The Campaign to Dump Dirty Diesel," "Pollution from Giant Livestock Farms Threatens Public Health," and "Pesticides Threaten Farm Children's Health."

Physicians for Social Responsibility (PSR)
1875 Connecticut Ave. NW, Suite 1012, Washington, DC 20009
(202) 667-4260 • fax: (202) 667-4201
e-mail: psrnatl@psr.org • Web site: www.psr.org

Founded in 1961, PSR documented the presence of strontium-90—a highly radioactive waste product of atmospheric nuclear testing—in American children's teeth. This finding led rapidly to the Limited Nuclear Test Ban treaty that ended above-ground explosions by the superpowers. PSR's mission is to address public health threats that affect people in the United States and around the world. The PSR Web site publishes fact sheets and article excerpts, including "Healthy Fish, Healthy Families" and "Asthma and the Role of Air Pollution."

Political Economy Research Center (PERC)
502 S. Nineteenth Ave., Suite 211, Bozeman, MT 59718
(406) 587-9591 • fax: (406) 586-7555
e-mail: perc@perc.org • Web site: www.perc.org

PERC is a nonprofit research and educational organization that seeks market-oriented solutions to environmental problems. Areas of research covered in the PERC Policy Series papers include endangered species, forestry, fisheries, mines, parks, public lands, property rights, hazardous waste, pollution, water, and wildlife. PERC conducts a variety of conferences, offers internships and fellowships, and provides environmental education materials. On its Web site PERC provides access to recent and archived articles, reports, and its policy series, including such titles as "Property Rights and Pesticides" and "Superfund: The Shortcut That Failed."

Worldwatch Institute
1776 Massachusetts Ave. NW, Washington, DC 20036-1904
(202) 452-1999 • fax: (202) 296-7368
e-mail: worldwatch@worldwatch.org
Web site: www.worldwatch.org

Worldwatch is a nonprofit public policy research organization dedicated to informing policymakers and the public about emerging global problems and trends and the complex links between the world economy and its environmental support systems. It publishes the bimonthly *World Watch* magazine, the Environmental Alert series, and several policy papers. Recent and archived issues of *World Watch* are available on its Web site.

Bibliography of Books

Rick Abraham — *The Dirty Truth: The Oil and Chemical Dependency of George W. Bush.* Houston, TX: Mainstream, 2000.

Terry L. Anderson, ed. — *Political Environmentalism: Going Behind the Green Curtain.* Stanford, CA: Hoover Institution Press, 2000.

Anthony L. Andrady, ed. — *Plastics and the Environment.* Hoboken, NJ: WileyInterscience, 2003.

Pamela S. Chasek, ed. — *The Global Environment in the Twenty-First Century: Prospects for International Cooperation.* Tokyo: United Nations University Press, 2000.

Nicholas P. Cheremisinoff — *Handbook of Pollution Prevention Practices.* New York: M. Dekker, 2001.

Biliana Cicin-Sain — *The Future of U.S. Ocean Policy: Choices for the New Century.* Washington, DC: Island Press, 2000.

Janet M. Currie — *Air Pollution and Infant Health: What Can We Learn from California's Recent Experience?* Cambridge, MA: National Bureau of Economic Research, 2004.

Terry Dinan and Christian Spoor — *An Evaluation of Cap-and-Trade Programs for Reducing U.S. Carbon Emissions.* Washington, DC: Congress of the United States, Congressional Budget Office, 2001.

Jack Doyle — *Taken for a Ride: Detroit's Big Three and the Politics of Pollution.* New York: Four Walls Eight Windows, 2000.

E. Melanie DuPuis, ed. — *Smoke and Mirrors: The Politics and Culture of Air Pollution.* New York: New York University Press, 2004.

Paul S. Fischbeck and R. Scott Farrow, eds. — *Improving Regulation: Cases in Environment, Health, and Safety.* Washington, DC: Resources for the Future, 2001.

R. Allan Freeze — *The Environmental Pendulum: A Quest for the Truth About Toxic Chemicals, Human Health, and Environmental Protection.* Berkeley: University of California Press, 2000.

Eddie J. Girdner — *Killing Me Softly: Toxic Waste, Corporate Profit, and the Struggle for Environmental Justice.* New York: Monthly Review Press, 2002.

Elizabeth Glass Geltman	*Recycling Land: Understanding the Legal Landscape of Brownfield Development.* Ann Arbor: University of Michigan Press, 2000.
Hugh S. Gorman	*Redefining Efficiency: Pollution Concerns, Regulatory Mechanisms, and Technological Change in the U.S. Petroleum Industry.* Akron, OH: University of Akron Press, 2001.
Charlotte Haynes	*Mission Possible: State Progress Controlling Runoff Under the Coastal Nonpoint Pollution Control Program.* Washington, DC: Coast Alliance, 2000.
Richard Hofrichter, ed.	*Toxic Struggles: The Theory and Practice of Environmental Justice.* Salt Lake City: University of Utah Press, 2002.
Ruediger Kuehr and Eric Williams, eds.	*Computers and the Environment: Understanding and Managing Their Impacts.* Boston: Kluwer Academic Publishers, 2003.
Saul Landau	*The Business of America: How Consumers Have Replaced Citizens and How We Can Reverse the Trend.* New York: Routledge, 2004.
Bjorn Lomborg	*The Skeptical Environmentalist: Measuring the Real State of the World.* Cambridge, UK: Cambridge University Press, 2001.
Gordon McGranahan and Frank Murray, eds.	*Air Pollution and Health in Rapidly Developing Countries.* Sterling, VA: Earthscan, 2003.
Gordon McGranahan et al.	*The Citizens at Risk: From Urban Sanitation to Sustainable Cities.* Sterling, VA: Earthscan, 2001.
Bob Mizon	*Light Pollution: Response and Remedies.* New York: Springer, 2002.
Gunter Pauli, J. Hugh Faulkner, and Fritjof Capra	*Upsizing: The Road to Zero Emissions, More Jobs, More Income and No Pollution.* Sheffield, England: Greenleaf, 2000.
Paul R. Portney and Robert N. Stavins, eds.	*Public Policies for Environmental Protection.* Washington, DC: Resources for the Future, 2000.
Joe Schilling, Christine Gaspar, and Nadejda Mishkovsky	*Beyond Fences: Brownfields and the Challenges of Land Use Controls.* Washington, DC: International City/County Management Association, 2000.
P.J. Simmons and Chantal de Jonge Oudraat, eds.	*Managing Global Issues: Lessons Learned.* Washington, DC: Carnegie Endowment for International Peace, 2001.
Clive L. Spash and Sandra McNally, eds.	*Managing Pollution: Economic Valuation and Environmental Toxicology.* Northampton, MA: E. Elgar, 2001.

| James Gustave Speth | *Red Sky at Morning: America and the Crisis of the Global Environment.* New Haven, CT: Yale University Press, 2004. |

| Richard L. Stroup and Roger E. Meiners, eds. | *Cutting Green Tape: Toxic Pollutants, Environmental Regulation, and the Law.* New Brunswick, NJ: Transaction Publishers, 2000. |

| Jacqueline Vaughn Switzer | *Environmental Politics: Domestic and Global Dimensions.* Boston: Bedford/St. Martin's, 2001. |

| Martyn Turner and Brian O'Connell | *The Whole World's Watching: Decarbonizing the Economy and Saving the World.* Chichester, England: John Wiley & Sons, 2001. |

| Adam S. Weinberg, David N. Pellow, and Allan Schnaiberg | *Urban Recycling and the Search for Sustainable Community Development.* Princeton, NJ: Princeton University Press, 2000. |

| David Wheeler | *Racing to the Bottom? Foreign Investment and Air Pollution in Developing Countries.* Washington, DC: World Bank, Development Research Group, Infrastructure and Environment, 2001. |

| B.C. Wolverton and John D. Wolverton | *Growing Clean Water: Nature's Solution to Water Pollution.* Picayune, MS: Wolverton Environmental Services, 2001. |

| World Bank Development Research Group | *Greening Industry: New Roles for Communities, Markets, and Governments.* Washington, DC: World Bank, 2000. |

Index